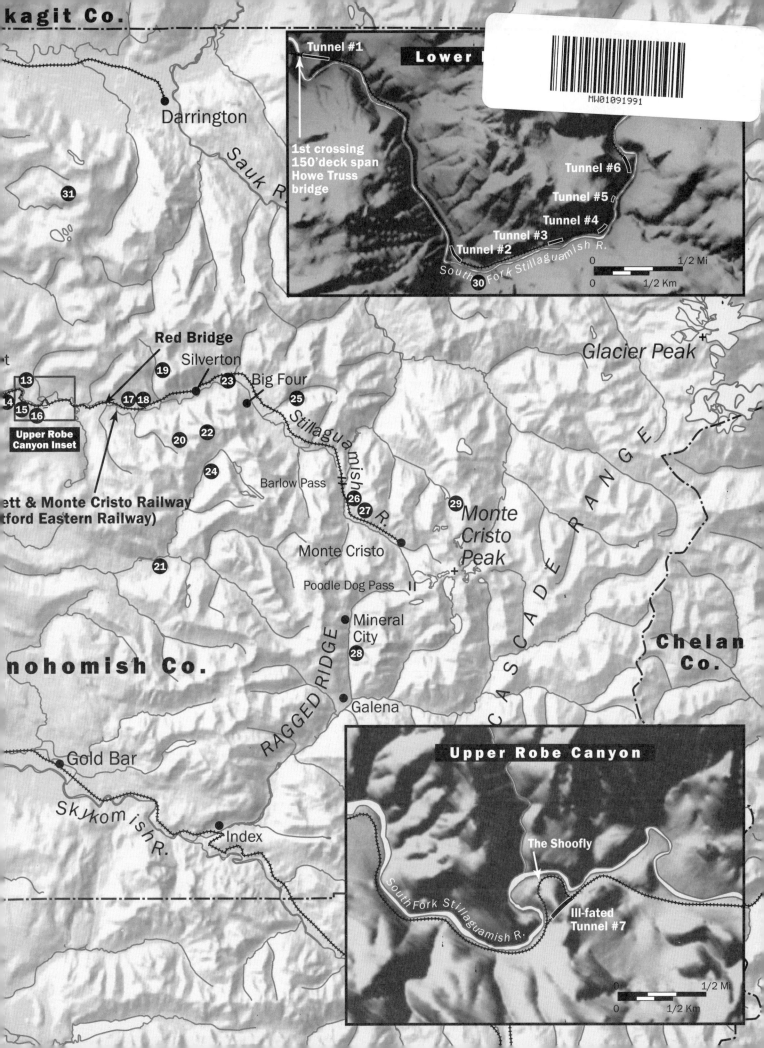

kagit Co.

Darrington

Sauk R.

31

Tunnel #1

Lower

1st crossing
150' deck span
Howe Truss
bridge

Tunnel #6
Tunnel #5
Tunnel #4
Tunnel #3
Tunnel #2

South Fork Stillaguamish R.

30

0   1/2 Mi
0   1/2 Km

Red Bridge

Silverton

19   23

Big Four

13

t

14

15

16

25

Glacier Peak

17 18

Upper Robe
Canyon Inset

Stillaguamish R.

20   22

ett & Monte Cristo Railway
tford Eastern Railway)

24

Barlow Pass

26
27

29 Monte
Cristo
Peak

C
A
S
C
A
D
E

R
A
N
G
E

Monte Cristo

21

Poodle Dog Pass

Chelan
Co.

R
A
G
G
E
D

R
I
D
G
E

Mineral
City

28

nohomish Co.

Galena

Gold Bar

Skykomish R.

Index

Upper Robe Canyon

The Shoofly

South Fork Stillaguamish R.

Ill-fated
Tunnel #7

0   1/2 Mi
0   1/2 Km

MW01091991

The Everett and Monte Cristo Railway

Phil Woodhouse, Daryl Jacobson, and Bill Petersen

Oso Publishing
C O M P A N Y

PUBLISHED BY
Oso Publishing Company
31328 N. Brooks Creek Road
Arlington, WA 98223

ISBN 0-9647521-8-2

Printed and bound in the United States of America

Manuscript editor: Ina Chang
Proofreader: Teri Kieffer
Indexer: Julie Kawabata
Editorial assistant: Jane Wyatt
Design and production: James D. Kramer design services, Everett, WA 98208

Table of Contents

Acknowledgments

The authors would like to express their sincere appreciation to Hancock Timber Resources, Mason Browne, Rivers Network, John Garner, the Snohomish County Council, County Executive Bob Drewel, Snohomish County Parks, the Stillaguamish Citizens Alliance, Steve and Nancy Dean, Enid Nordlund, Bob Thorsen, Sue Doroff, Phil Wallin, former state senator Kevin Quigley, and the many people who have donated their time and money to the work parties that have built trails and cleaned up Robe Canyon Park.

The publisher would like to sincerely thank the following people for their generous assistance: Peter Selvig of the United States Forest Service, Margaret Riddle and David Dilgard of the Everett Public Library, Dr. David Cameron, Larry Schrenk, Walt and John Taubeneck, Warren Wing, Steve Hauff, Dan Cozine, and Didrik Voss.

1

A Land Rich in Resources

After the end of the Civil War in 1865, people began pushing westward along the trails from the Mississippi and Missouri rivers to the West Coast. Many followed the Oregon Trail to the mostly unmapped Pacific Northwest to seek their fortunes. The few non-native settlements in the region were located on the shores of rivers, streams, lakes, and other navigable waterways. So dense were the forests that a person could walk several hundred yards into them and become completely lost. The trees grew to heights of over 400 feet and were closely spaced, creating a dim netherworld on the forest floor. For this reason, travel generally took place on the water, and clearing land for agriculture was slow and difficult work. By 1880, the population of what was to become Snohomish County was listed as 4,262 souls.

The timber industry was the first to exploit the area. The lumber companies established a mill at the water's edge and worked their way into the forest from the shore. Gradually, the land was opened. Trappers worked on trap lines along the

Looking north on Chestnut at Hewitt Avenue in January 1892. Mud was clearly the predominant paving at the time. Everett ultimately became the terminus of the Everett and Monte Cristo Railway, which connected with other railways such as the Seattle & Montana. Frank LaRoche took this photo for the Everett Land Company. *(Enid Nordlund Collection, Frank LaRoche photo)*

Looking west on Hewitt Avenue from Market Street in March 1892. Named for Henry Hewitt, a wealthy owner of Wisconsin timberland and one of the early prime movers of Everett, this east-west thoroughfare is still one of the main streets of downtown Everett. Hewitt joined forces with Colby and Hoyt (who also have Everett streets named after them) to establish the land company that planned the city. *(Enid Nordlund Collection, King and Baskerville Studio photo)*

Poodle Dog Pass Looking West, Monte Cristo, Wash.

Silvertip Peak forms the backdrop for this winter scene viewed from 4,200-foot Poodle Dog Pass. The pass, named after the nearby Poodle Dog Mine Claim, carries the Silver Lake Trail from the watershed of the South Fork of the Sauk River to the watershed of Silver Creek to the south. *(John A. Juleen photo)*

waterways that led into the Cascades, and a trickle of prospectors followed. Whispers of gold and other valuable metals began to circulate throughout the region as samples of ore were brought down from the hills. Many of the early settlers discovered that little work was available, so they decided to try their hand at mineral prospecting.

Only a few people actually knew the art of locating minerals. One such prospector was a young man named Joseph Pearsall. Although Pearsall held a prominent position with a mining and smelting firm in northern Idaho, his first love was the thrill of discovery, which led him to climb where few mountain goats would tread, let alone other men. One such venture in the early summer of 1889 took him along the east side of Silver Creek, northeast of what is now Index, Washington, where prospectors were searching for galena, silver, and gold in the red mineral-stained valley. Tracing a mineral vein up toward the crest of Hubbart's Peak, he stopped at a lofty perch near the north peak. Looking across a ridge and down into the confluence of two valleys, he noticed a "broad, glittering streak" on the mountain that, when viewed with his field glasses, he was certain was galena, the sulfide ore of lead. The galena in this area was known to also contain silver, and investigation in the surrounding area revealed gold.

A bird's-eye view of the new town of Everett in the 1890s. The tracks of the 3S Railway are in the lower right of the photo, where they cross the Snohomish River at Lowell. The swing bridge over the river is in the open position. In the distance are the steel bargeworks and the Sumner Iron Works along the banks of the river and the nailworks on Port Gardner Bay. *(Everett Public Library Collection)*

The first claim was staked in the valley on July 4, 1889. By the summer of 1890, the rush was on, and many more claims had been staked in the valley and even high on the surrounding mountain peaks. Fred Wilmans, an associate of Joseph Pearsall, named the area Monte Cristo after Alexandre Dumas's *Count of Monte Cristo* because he felt the name exuded wealth and mystery.

The mining camp of Monte Cristo began to take shape as more claims were staked. But transportation to the remote area was difficult, both because of distance and because hiking over a crude trail was the only way in. Monte Cristo was in a deep canyon surrounded in almost every direction by mountains up to 7,000 feet in elevation. It lay at the junction of two creeks that formed at that point the headwaters of the South Fork of the Sauk River, but the Sauk was too shallow and rocky to accommodate steamboat traffic. Later, a puncheon road was built up the Sauk River to the camp, but even this wasn't enough to supply the growing demands of the new mining area. Also, the ore was refractory, which meant that processing it would require heavy milling equipment. An effective mining operation would also require a sawmill and some means of transporting the huge quantities of rich ore from the mines to a smelter. All of these factors kept a potential boom at bay.

The office of the Everett Land Company, which was started by the Colby-Hoyt-Hewitt people who founded Everett. Everett was one of the few "planned cities" of the time that actually developed into a viable town. Francis Brownell, whose law office was also in this building, served as an attorney for many of the fledgling firms in the area. *(Everett Public Library Collection)*

Meanwhile, local businessmen in Snohomish and other towns watched with interest as the transcontinental Great Northern Railway extended its lines toward Puget Sound. The Northern Pacific Railroad already had a tidewater terminus in Tacoma; the Great Northern was looking for a spot farther north. Charles Colby and Colgate Hoyt, members of the Northern Pacific's executive committee, traveled to the Northwest to see how they might personally cash in on the economic boom that the new Great Northern terminus would bring. They planned to quietly buy up all the available land near the likely terminus, and then, when plans were announced, they would see their property skyrocket in value.

Colby and Hoyt had heard that Great Northern surveyors were already at work in the Skagit River Valley. They reasoned that the railway would therefore reach tidewater near the small town of Anacortes, and they began buying property in that area. Their plans leaked out, however, and savvy landowners quickly raised property prices to exorbitant levels—as much as $5,000 an acre. Their plan unveiled, Colby and Hoyt retreated to regroup.

While mulling over their dilemma, Colby and Hoyt met Henry Hewitt of Tacoma, who knew the region and had prospered in the timber business and other endeavors. The three men became friends and sailed off on a trip to Alaska to unwind and to discuss business. Hewitt owned land near the tiny settlement of Port Gardner on Port Gardner Bay, about 30 miles north of Seattle. Since Port Gardner Bay was navigable and a suitable anchorage for large ships, he suggested that they buy land in that area and wait to see what developed.

Colby and Hoyt bought much of the property on the peninsula where Port Gardner was located. Fortunately for them, the Great Northern was extended down the west slope of the Cascades through the Skykomish River Valley, making Port Gardner the most likely tidewater terminal. This time, their plan stayed under wraps. They created the Colby-Hoyt Syndicate and set about planning a city on Port Gardner Bay that would feature broad streets, ample lots, and industries to employ the inhabitants. It would have a steel nailworks, a paper mill, a steel bargeworks, and a brick plant. One evening over dinner, Colby and Hewitt were discussing what to name their new town, and as dessert was served, Colby's young son, Everett, asked for seconds. The men remarked that the lad always wanted the best of everything that was offered, just as they wanted the best for their new venture. They decided to name the town Everett.

Meanwhile, the promising Monte Cristo mines were consolidated by the Wilmans-Bond Group—John, Fred, and Steve Wilmans; Leigh Hunt; Judge Hiram Bond; and Ed Blewett. These Northwest-based men knew that a railroad would be required to haul massive machinery into the area and to transport the resulting ore concentrates out. They were respected and wealthy men, but a railroad from Everett to Monte Cristo was far beyond their financial means, so they began seeking additional capital.

The group considered several routes for transporting ore: One would be by riverboat from Everett to Sauk City (Rockport) and then by rail or trail to Monte Cristo. Another would be by rail from Everett to Index and up the North Fork of the Skykomish to Silver Creek, and then by switchback trail over Poodle Dog Pass or a tunnel to Monte Cristo. This route would be extremely expensive and also ill-advised because the extent of the mineral deposits in the Silver Creek area was still unknown. (The idea might have originated with people involved in the Everett Land Company or the Monte Cristo Mines who already had mining claims in the Silver Creek area. Talk of a railroad up Silver Creek would have raised the value of their holdings considerably.) Another proposed route would run a rail line up the South Fork of the Stillaguamish River, over or through the divide between the headwaters of that river and the South Fork of the Sauk, and then to Monte Cristo and possibly Silver Creek. Still another route would use the Seattle, Lake Shore & Eastern tracks to Arlington and then run along the North Fork of the Stillaguamish River to Darrington.

The Wilmans-Bond Group, which had purchased Joe Pearsall's interest in the claims, learned of the efforts near Port Gardner Bay and approached the Colby-Hoyt Syndicate. They suggested that the syndicate build a railroad between the Monte Cristo area and the future town of Everett on Port Gardner Bay and enter the mining and smelting industry. Hoyt convinced his good friend John D. Rockefeller to put up enough money to build a railroad, a smelter, and a concentrator.

John D. Rockefeller, Sr. (left), titan of American industry and primary financial backer of the Everett and Monte Cristo Railway and his associate Frederick T. Gates (right) who oversaw Rockefeller's far-flung investments. *(Rockefeller Archive Center)*

The contract proposed by the Wilmans-Bond Group called for the Colby-Hoyt Syndicate to build a standard-gauge railroad—at an estimated cost of $1 million—that would transport 500 tons of ore 24 hours a day (except Sundays) and handle all freight and passengers connected with the mining operation. If this was accomplished by January 1, 1893, the Wilmans-Bond Group would develop the mines to a capacity of 500 tons of ore a day and allow the railway to transport all the freight to and from the mines for 15 years. They would pay the railroad 3 cents per ton for each mile of haul. If the ore exceeded an average of 500 tons per day over a six-month period, the fee would drop to $2\frac{1}{2}$ cents per ton for each mile. If the ore exceeded 1,000 tons per day over six months, the rate would be 2 cents per ton for each mile.

The Wilmans-Bond Group also proposed to form a mining corporation and issue stock in the mining properties. Under the proposed contract, one-fourth of the mining stock would be exchanged for one-fourth of the railroad stock. Both companies would have to be free of debt at the time of stock transfers.

Colby sought the advice of a mining engineer named Alton Dickerman, who was associated with Rockefeller. Dickerman estimated the length of the railroad at 60 miles and computed the output of the mines at only 350 tons per day. At the time there was little geological knowledge of the Cascade Mountains and after a personal inspection Dickerman was privately skeptical about the potential of the mining properties, which had hardly been developed. Monte Cristo itself had only two log cabins. Publicly, however, he protected his corporate affiliation and issued glowing reports: Dickerman estimated that by January 1, 1893, there would be 5,000 people in the mining camp. He concluded that the opportunity was "exceptional," that the returns would be large, and that the risk was much less than with most mining propositions because of the quantity and quality of the ore. Dickerman calculated that even if only 350 tons of ore were shipped per day, the railroad would still clear $70,200 per year because of merchandise, passengers, and mail.

On February 3, 1892, the Wilmans-Bond Group and the Colby-Hoyt Syndicate finalized the contract. The new rail line was to branch off the main line of the Seattle Lake Shore and Eastern Railway, the Seattle & Montana Railway, or both. The final contract differed from the proposed one in that the freight fees would be 5 cents per ton per mile, to

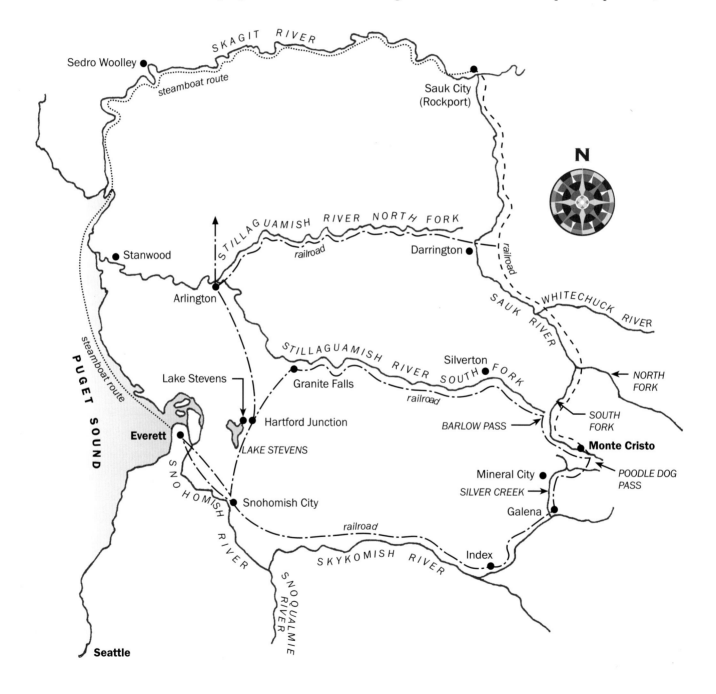

Proposed routes for the new railroad.

be shipped in 5-ton lots (except blasting powder, because they didn't want to encourage large shipments of explosives). Charges for freight and blasting powder shipped in lots of less than 5 tons would be at "fair and reasonable" rates. The final agreement also made no mention of trading railroad stock for mining stock because on December 10, 1891, the two groups had signed an agreement that put the major mines at Monte Cristo in the hands of Colby and Hoyt.

As for the possible routes for the new railroad, two were seriously considered. The longer route would be along the Seattle Lake Shore and Eastern from Snohomish to Arlington, along the North Fork of the Stillaguamish to the Sauk (where Darrington is now located), and then along the "Pioneer Trail" to Monte Cristo. The second route would follow the Seattle Lake Shore and Eastern as far as Hartford and then follow the Pilchuck River to Granite Falls and up the South Fork of the Stillaguamish to Monte Cristo. The latter route, while shorter, would have to cross the divide between the Stillaguamish Valley and the Sauk River Valley.

While surveying from the Monte Cristo end, near the divide between the South Fork of

The mining interests in Everett often wined and dined special guests at the Monte Cristo Hotel, which is shown here during construction in the summer of 1892. The hotel had a ballroom, a dining hall, and guest rooms (with bathrooms down the hall). In 1904, the hotel was sold to the Sisters of Providence and became Providence Hospital. When a new hospital building was later erected, the old hotel became an outpatient clinic. It maintained this function well past the middle of the century but was eventually torn down. *(Enid Nordlund Collection; photographer unknown, but possibly Herman Siewart)*

the Stillaguamish River and the South Fork of the Sauk River, Chief Engineer M. Q. Barlow noticed a small stream at the base of a large cliff. The stream didn't appear to flow into the Sauk River, as others in the area did. Barlow found that the spring actually emptied into a narrow valley to the west. This led to his discovery that the two valleys were linked by a low pass (soon named Barlow Pass) and that the narrow valley was the upper headwaters of the South Fork of the Stillaguamish River. This meant that a rail line could be easily routed through the pass, thus eliminating the need for a tunnel or a switchback over the divide. The recent discovery of iron deposits near Mount Pilchuck and gold and silver strikes at Camp Independence (Silverton) also made the pass the preferred route. The Sauk River plan was quickly abandoned in favor of the South Fork Stillaguamish plan.

On March 11, 1892, the new railroad company was incorporated as the Everett and Monte Cristo Railway Company. It was capitalized at $1.8 million.

First Street and Avenue D in Snohomish City, looking east. In this town, the Everett and Monte Cristo trains switched from the east-west 3S trackage to the north-south Seattle Lake Shore and Eastern trackage, which took them to Hartford Junction. At Hartford Junction, they switched onto their own tracks for the 42.1-mile remainder of the trip to Monte Cristo. *(Everett Public Library Collection, Palace Floating Gallery photo)*

The 3S Railway

In 1889, some Port Gardner and Snohomish City businessmen began to worry that the Great Northern, which was heading west over the Cascades, would not make Everett the tidewater terminus but would instead continue to Seattle or Tacoma. This prompted the men to form a railroad corporation called the Snohomish, Skykomish, and Spokane Railway and Transportation Company. The 3S, as they called it, would run from Port Gardner Bay to the Cascade Mountains. There it would join with the Great Northern, thus assuring that Port Gardner would be the tidewater terminus. The company was incorporated on April 19, 1889, and bonds were sold to finance the construction. The company obtained the necessary right-of-way and began building the extension from Snohomish City to Port Gardner Bay on July 16, 1891.

Soon 200 men worked on the grade, which was expected to be completed within three months. Tracklaying began on October 1, 1891, west from Snohomish City. (Some track was laid in an easterly direction because the line was also expected to tap the Silver Creek mining district, but nothing substantial ever became of this.) Construction to Lowell, a distance of 7 miles, was completed in March 1892. However, because of financing problems, the railroad was never operated and the trackage was sold to the Everett Land Company (a Colby, Hoyt, and Hewitt company). Because the right-of-way and other holdings were already in order for the 3S Railway, the Everett Land Company wasted no time in selling its holdings in this line to the Everett and Monte Cristo Railway (also a Colby-Hoyt company) for $400,000.

The telegraph office of the 3S Railway on Pacific Avenue near Chestnut in Everett in April 1892. The Everett and Monte Cristo Railway purchased the tracks of the 3S to gain access to Snohomish City where, via the Seattle Lake Shore and Eastern, they could reach their own tracks at Hartford Junction. *(Everett Public Library Collection, King and Baskerville Studio photo)*

The Howe truss swing bridge at Lowell that carried the 3S tracks over the Snohomish River at Lowell. This photo was taken January 14, 1892. *(Everett Public Library Collection, Frank LaRoche photo)*

Three gentlemen pose on a partially turned Howe truss swing bridge in the 1890s. This might have been the Everett and Monte Cristo's swing bridge where the line crossed the Snohomish River at Lowell. The low bridge, which had to be moved to accommodate boat traffic on the navigable waterway, was originally built to carry the 3S Railway but was sold to the Everett and Monte Cristo before a single train had crossed it. *(Phil Woodhouse Collection)*

The Northern Pacific #309 at Lowell in June 1892. It is shown here hauling pulp logs; note that the flat car is still lettered for the Seattle Lake Shore & Eastern Railway. This locomotive was leased from the Northern Pacific for use as the construction locomotive on the 3S line. *(Everett Public Library Collection, King & Baskerville Photo, #096)*

2

Construction Begins

The Everett and Monte Cristo Railway construction plan called for a telegraph line along the right-of-way and a wagon road along the entire length of the line from Hartford or Getchell to Monte Cristo. Grading for the railroad commenced at Granite Falls in April 1892. In the meantime, work on the 3S portion between Lowell and Snohomish City continued, with rails reaching Lowell and crossing the new bridge over the Snohomish River on April 14. In May, the Great Northern made arrangements with the Everett and Monte Cristo to use the former 3S tracks between Snohomish City and Everett in anticipation of completing their line over Stevens Pass.

During the Colby-Hoyt syndicate's negotiations with Rockefeller's New York syndicate, the parties agreed to allow Seattle businessman H. C.

After the railway was completed, goods destined for the Penn Mining Company's camp at Goat Lake were shipped up to Barlow Pass and placed in a warehouse. This trusty wagon crew would transport the goods to the camp along a 6-mile coarse puncheon road. Goods destined for the mine itself were hauled past the camp to Goat Lake, taken by barge to the head of the lake, and then dragged 1,300 feet of elevation up a snowfield to the mine, high on the side of Cadet Peak below Osceola Pass. *(Enid Nordlund Collection)*

The nailworks and warehouse under construction at Everett in October 1891. The businesses along this stretch of Puget Sound were later served by both rail and ship. The tracks in the foreground belong to the Seattle & Montana Railway. *(Everett Public Library Collection, Frank LaRoche photo)*

Henry to build the railroad using routes, plans, and prices determined by the Rockefeller interests in consultation with Charles Colby and F. N. Finney of Milwaukee, who would be in charge of construction. In addition, Henry would be required to contribute $100,000 to any syndicate organized by Colby and Hoyt to construct the railroad.

In March, copper had been discovered along the right-of-way just 2 miles east of Granite Falls. This discovery became the Wayside Mine, which for many years was the deepest shaft mine in Washington. A vertical shaft, horizontal tunnel, and mill building were built within spitting distance of passing trains.

Barlow and 30 surveyors completed the final location surveys along the South Fork of the Stillaguamish toward Monte Cristo, and 75 men worked on the wagon road along the railroad right-of-way. The *Everett Herald* predicted that 4,000 men would soon be at work building the line. Fearing violence and racketeering along the routes of the Great Northern and the Everett and Monte Cristo, the Snohomish County commissioners refused to issue liquor licenses along the rights-of-way.

Barlow was ordered to "push the road as fast as money and labor would allow." He estimated that construction would be finished by December, but workers were hard to come by because many stayed only long enough to get a paycheck or two and then moved on to greener pastures. The company scoured the cities and towns along Puget Sound, but labor remained scarce. Italian immigrant laborers provided much of the manpower. (Contrary to popular lore, Chinese labor was never used.)

By early May, final locations were being made as fast as snow conditions would allow. The tote road was pushed with vigor, using split cedar planks, as if the road were to be permanent. A stage line made regular runs over it, delivering men and supplies. Frequent rainstorms and lack of manpower hampered road building on both the Everett and Monte Cristo and the Great Northern lines, while in Everett the Colby-Hoyt Syndicate focused on plans for the big, new smelter. The only question left was whether the railroad would run north or south of the city. The *Everett Herald* reported on June 9 that a large depot would be built in Everett on the south side of Hewitt Avenue between McDougall Street and Broadway. The new building would be used by the Great Northern, the Everett and Monte Cristo, and the Seattle & Montana. It had originally been

The Hartford Hotel in Hartford Junction, where the tracks left the Seattle Lake Shore and Eastern line and headed east into the hills. *(Lake Stevens Historical Society Collection)*

Survey crews and graders in late 1892 or early summer 1893, prepare the grade for tracks between Barlow Pass and Twin Bridges. Tracklayers were close behind. *(Enid Nordlund Collection)*

planned for the north side of Hewitt, but the tracks curved there, rendering the site unsuitable. Ultimately, the Monte Cristo depot was built near the eastern end of Pacific Avenue.

A construction engineers' camp during the building of the Everett and Monte Cristo line. The photographer probably stood on a portion of the right-of-way. Surveyors led the way through the wilderness and were followed by construction engineers and their crews, who graded the line by filling or cutting the terrain. When fill and cut techniques failed, they used trestling or bridging. The engineers' camps, which consisted of tents and wagons, were constantly on the move. *(The Northwest Magazine, February 1895)*

The first rails—13 carloads of them—arrived on July 10, 1892, on the Northern Pacific. Some were used to complete the connection of the Great Northern and 3S at Everett, and the rest were delivered to Hartford Junction. The arrival of the first shipment of rails was a proud moment, as was the arrival of the first locomotive for the line, dubbed Engine #1. It was a $68\frac{1}{2}$-ton Ten Wheeler with 21-by-26-inch cylinders built by Cooke and Company of Paterson, New Jersey. It made its first run out of Snohomish on August 5. Engine #2, an identical locomotive, arrived the following week.

To help finance the railway, bonds were issued in denominations of $1,000, with a maximum issue of 3,000 bonds, or $3 million. The bonds were to pay annual interest of 7 percent and would come due in 50 years.

The Trout Stream in the Canyon

Of the 42 miles of right-of-way from Hartford to Monte Cristo, the most controversial and challenging was the 5 miles in Robe Canyon just east of Granite Falls. This deep, winding chasm with high, perpendicular walls of solid rock remains a tribute to one of the biggest blunders in Northwest railroading history. When Barlow's survey crews reached this area,

Along the Scenic Railway to Big Four Inn

The Stillaguamish River's Robe Canyon viewed from next to tunnel #1 on the Monte Cristo line, looking up the tracks toward Robe. The rail traveler would have just passed over a 150-foot deck span Howe truss bridge and through tunnel #1. This photo was one of many taken by John A. Juleen and made into postcards. *(Phil Woodhouse Collection, John A. Juleen photo)*

A section of the Stillaguamish River's South Fork known as Silver Rapids in Robe Canyon. A fellow stands on the railroad right-of-way at the upper left of the photo. Reports about the canyon were often greatly exaggerated—the cliffs were said to be thousands of feet high. *(Phil Woodhouse Collection, Herman Siewart photo)*

the settlers warned that the stream, while tranquil during the dry season, could become a raging, destructive torrent. With a heavy snow pack in the mountains and a warm Chinook wind out of the southwest, the river could rise several feet in a short time. (A "Chinook wind" means different things in different parts of the country. In Western Washington, a Chinook is a warm, wet wind from the southwest in November and December and is now often called the "Pineapple Express" because it originates in the area of the Hawaiian Islands.)

With this warning in mind, Barlow began surveying a long, circuitous route around the canyon, above the upper end of the chasm where the terrain mellows out. This route would eliminate the danger of flood damage to the road. Barlow's decision was quickly challenged by the syndicate members, who considered the Stillaguamish River a small trout stream compared to rivers in the East and the Midwest, along which great railroads had been built. They trusted their

The western portal of tunnel #1 viewed from a low bank along the Stillaguamish River. The loose, unstable soil at this portion of the bore collapsed whenever the supporting timbers caught fire. The Howe truss bridge that was the first crossing over the river is in the foreground. *(Norm Birger, Geology of the Southwestern Portion of the Stillaguamish Quadrangle, [University of Washington thesis, 1910]; courtesy of Steve and Nancy Dean)*

In the 1920s, a Hartford Eastern gas car emerges from tunnel #1 onto the Howe truss bridge several miles above Granite Falls. *(Enid Nordlund Collection)*

(right) Mount Pilchuck provides the backdrop to bridge #18 on the Everett and Monte Cristo Railway. When first constructed, this bridge was a double throughspan Howe truss bridge with each span measuring 126 feet. After the devastating flood of 1897, the river was diverted and channeled to allow for a single 126-foot throughspan Howe truss bridge. This photo was taken between 1894 and 1897, probably by Herman Siewart, official photographer for the railway. *(Phil Woodhouse Collection)*

A double-span Howe truss bridge near Everett. This might have been the Everett and Monte Cristo's second crossing of the Stillaguamish River near Robe. Each section of the second crossing bridge spanned 126 feet. Howe truss bridges were among the first engineered bridges in which members that carried tension forces were made of steel and members that carried compressive forces were made of wood. *(Enid Nordlund Collection)*

railroad men more than the local settlers and decided that the long, circuitous route would be too expensive and time consuming. They opted instead for the shortest, most expedient route—up the canyon.

With the route established, Finney awarded the prime construction contract to Henry and Balch, as had been agreed upon during the Colby-Hoyt negotiations with the Rockefeller syndicate. (Balch was Henry's business partner but not a syndicate member.) Henry and Balch, in turn, offered subcontracts to other local concerns to do the work on the 3S portion of the line as well as the line itself from Hartford Junction on the Seattle Lake Shore and Eastern to Monte Cristo. Henry and Balch thus made a profit without doing any of the work themselves.

In July 1892, work began on three bridges across the Stillaguamish. (See figure below.) The first bridge was a 150-foot deck span Howe truss bridge at the lower end of the canyon. The second, above the upper end of the canyon at a site known as Rotary, consisted of two linked 126-foot throughspans, also of the Howe truss design. The third, $9^{1}/_{2}$ miles farther up the river at a spot now known as Red Bridge, was also a 126-foot Howe truss throughspan.

In the canyon proper, workers bored six tunnels. The first one, 847 feet long, was at the eastern end of the first bridge, on the downstream end of the canyon. The second was about $1^{1}/_{2}$ miles upstream and was 160 feet long. The last four were close together near the upper entrance to the canyon. Tunnel #3 was 250 feet long and just before Tunnel #4. Tunnel #4 was 140 feet long, and Tunnel #5 was 95 feet long. Tunnel #6 was the farthest upstream, 2,000 feet from the canyon's mouth, and was 277 feet long. A telegraph line was placed on poles along the line, allowing "the front" to remain in contact with the outside world. The Sunset Telephone Company also planned a line all the way into Monte Cristo to provide long-distance service.

In early July, a forest fire destroyed one of the engineering camps. All of the crew's personal belongings were lost, but field notes and instruments were saved. Rockfalls, cave-ins, and bad weather also combined to torment the crews in the canyon.

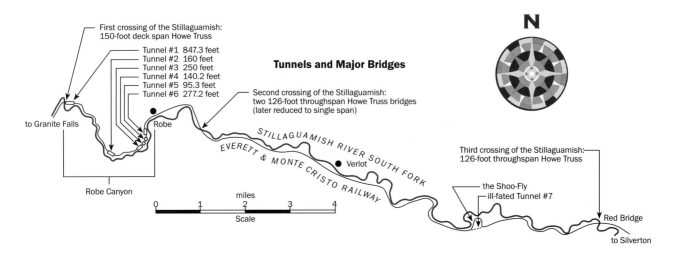

Key bridges and tunnels of the Everett and Monte Cristo Railway.

Tunnel #2 years before it was blasted into an open cut. This scene is in Robe Canyon looking back toward Granite Falls. Notice the men in the foreground and the wooden structure to the right of the tunnel portal. A cable has just been drawn across the Stillaguamish River. This photo might document the setting of the first cable for a suspension bridge across the river. The bridge carried a surface ore tramway for hauling limestone from a quarry on the left (south) side of the river to the railroad. The wooden structure became part of the bridge as it crossed above the tracks. *(Enid Nordlund Collection)*

Tunnel #5 in the 1890s. The railroad ran through Robe Canyon on log cribbing such as that shown in this photo. When the Stillaguamish River reached flood stage, it often ripped this cribbing and its roadbed from the canyon wall. After the Northern Pacific bought the line, it filled much of the vulnerable cribbing with concrete. *(Enid Nordlund Collection)*

Hardware for the Railroad

The hardware for the Monte Cristo line—5,000 tons of rails, fishplates, and spikes—arrived from the East Coast on several ships. They sailed around Cape Horn from Philadelphia, saving $30,000 compared to overland shipping.

The first seaborne shipment was originally to be offloaded in Seattle and delivered over the Seattle Lake Shore and Eastern to Hartford Junction. But since the connection of the 3S line with the Seattle & Montana was already completed, the ships could dock at Everett's Hewitt Avenue wharf and take the shorter route from Everett to Hartford.

Pile driving had begun on an extension of the wharf. The first two 10-wheel locomotives were put into official service on August 4, 1892. They had been shipped overland from the manufacturer in Paterson, New Jersey, in pieces, assembled in Seattle by engineer and fitter W. S. Boyd at the Northern Pacific roundhouse, and run to Everett on July 23 by Boyd over the Seattle Lake Shore and Eastern tracks. They weighed 68½ tons each and were powered by 21-by-26-inch cylinders. One was sent to Hartford, and the other was put to work as a construction train in Everett.

The spot in Robe Canyon where tunnel #4 was later bored. Taken in May 1892, the photo shows the rough terrain of the canyon. The rock in this area proved to be very unstable, and a series of collapses at tunnel #4 took the lives of several railroad workers. The roof of the tunnel was removed in 1911, ending the problem. *(Walt Meglassen Collection, Herman Siewart photo)*

A construction crew in 1892 in Robe Canyon between tunnel #1 and tunnel #2. This photo looks down the tracks toward Granite Falls. These men were probably Italian immigrants. Notice that the riprap rock has been laid by hand on flatcars to be hauled to the work site. Little power machinery was to be had in the 1890s. *(Phil Woodhouse Collection)*

Tunnel #6 before the log cribbing that supported the tracks was cased in concrete. During flood season, the Stillaguamish River would flow through this tunnel and tear out the rails for nearly a quarter-mile. Debris would also be jammed in the timbers within the tunnel. When the cribbing was set in concrete, the timbering was removed from the tunnel to allow floating material to pass through more easily. *(Enid Nordlund Collection)*

During the second week of June, the Rucker brothers, the Everett and Monte Cristo Railway, and Henry Hewitt signed an agreement on the tunnel and right-of-way that was to run under Everett. It stated that the tunnel would be 26 feet wide and bricked or stoned. It was to be strong enough to allow for construction of buildings over it. There would be two tracks, and the tunnel would start at Oakes Street on the east and exit at

The Wild West

Even though it was illegal to sell alcohol along the line, whiskey peddlers and some local ranchers took the risk and offered the much-desired spirits. Some enterprising souls actually erected large tents and even buildings to cater to the 1,500 to 2,000 workmen along the line (800 of whom worked in the 5-mile stretch of canyon). These establishments provided not only alcohol but also gambling, dancing, and women of questionable repute. Some of these entrepreneurs took advantage of the laborers along the line, many of whom were Italian immigrants who spoke little or no English. They cheated them at cards, overcharged for liquor and girls, and in some cases, after getting them thoroughly intoxicated, brutally robbed them.

After a while, enough was enough and one night a large group of laborers took up the matter in true Old West style. Armed with clubs, knives, and dynamite, they marched to one of the dives, a saloon and dance hall called the Monte Cristo Club 5 miles east of Granite Falls. They dynamited the bar and demolished the fixtures. The occupants, who were sleeping in the back room, miraculously escaped injury. At the Branch of the Burning Bush, another dive along the line, a mob of about 100 laborers warned the proprietors that if they didn't get out of the area, the same fate would befall them. The proprietors heeded the warning and promptly departed.

Another incident involved two woodcutters who were falling trees above a camp occupied by Italian laborers. They made their cuts so the trees would fall uphill, away from the workmen's camp. However, one tree rolled down the hill toward the camp. One of the woodcutters fled as the tree crashed into the camp, injuring two men. The second woodcutter descended the hillside to explain the accident and offer help. But one of the laborers, thinking that the act was intentional, picked up a Winchester rifle and pursued the woodcutter down the railroad grade. The fleeing man arrived at the camp of one of the survey parties, which was abandoned except for the bride of a civil engineer from Chicago. The lady hid him under the bed, took up her own Winchester, and waited at the tent door for the enraged laborer. When the laborer arrived, he quickly spotted the woodcutter cowering under the bed and raised his rifle to shoot. But the brave woman leveled her rifle at him and warned, "Now, you shoot and I'll shoot." He lowered his weapon and walked sullenly back to his companions.

This photo was obviously posed, but it illustrates the way people obtained merchandise in the 1890s. The building and its roof were constructed of hand-split shakes. Note the gold pan, boots, and shovels. The sacks probably contained flour and the boxes probably held shoes or boots.

Norton Street. It would be built by the Great Northern in 18 months at a cost of about $250,000. The Everett and Monte Cristo would pay trackage rights to Great Northern for use of the bore.

The Everett and Monte Cristo's locomotive #3, probably in 1893. Notice the link-and-pin coupler on the pilot beam, which had not yet been changed to a Gould Knuckle coupler. Use of the Gould couplers was a matter of pride for the railway, which claimed to be the first mainline railway to be completely equipped with the new devices. The material being hauled is probably rails, ties, and fishplates for construction of the line. *(Railroad Museum of Pennsylvania)*

About 1,500 men went to work building the road, and Everett and Monte Cristo General Manager F. N. Finney estimated that the road would be finished in November. Travelers to and from the mines and communities along the right-of-way began to extol the beauty and spectacular scenery along the route.

Along the line east of Hartford, compressed air drills worked at the east end of tunnel #1 in the canyon. The wagon road along the right-of-way was said to be the finest corduroy road in the county, allowing a 4-ton wagonload to be hauled over it by a four-horse team.

Rumors continued to circulate that the Everett and Monte Cristo would not stop at Monte Cristo but would continue over the mountains to the Okanogan. With all the mining, cattle, and agricultural traffic from east of the mountains, the continuation seemed

The Rucker Brothers

Wyatt and Bethel Rucker were key players during the entire lifetime of the Everett and Monte Cristo Railway. Wyatt, a successful Ohio businessman, ventured west in the spring of 1888 with his mother and his brother Bethel, and they initially settled in Tacoma. Wyatt determined that the Port Gardner area offered the most investment potential, so he began to invest and saw his holdings expand rapidly.

Over the years, the Rucker brothers became involved in logging, farming, milling, banking, and real estate. They built a large lumber mill at Lake Stevens and a smaller mill near Silverton, and they had significant timber interests in the area. Because these operations relied heavily on the railroad, the Rucker brothers were very concerned when the Monte Cristo branch of the Northern Pacific began to fail. To protect their interests, they leased the line from the Northern Pacific in 1915, ostensibly to continue the rail link that was so vital to their business interests. However, they were also required to maintain the railway as a common carrier, which meant that they had to continue freight and passenger service along the line. To meet this requirement, they replaced the freight and passenger locomotives with gas cars, which were cheaper to operate and required less substantial trackage, and renamed the line the Hartford Eastern Railway.

In 1925, the Ruckers bought the line outright. Things began to go downhill shortly thereafter. The timber industry was lagging, the Hartford Eastern did not have the funds to maintain its infrastructure, and ridership and freight shipments were declining. This, coupled with the severe winters, storms, flooding, and increasing competition from trucks and motor cars, led to the demise of the Hartford Eastern and the Rucker brothers' withdrawal from the area.

The Ruckers had a penchant for painting everything they owned white, including their mill buildings and the gas cars along the Hartford Eastern. One notable exception was gas car #25, Wyatt Rucker's personal car. The black Mitchell automobile, which was equipped with flanged wheels, was known locally as the "Black Mariah" after a New York paddy wagon.

The Black Mariah at Monte Cristo in 1918.
Wyatt Rucker stands at the center of the group.
(Washington State Historical Society)

The Everett and Monte Cristo's first locomotive, which was put to work as a construction train in Everett. *(Railroad Museum of Pennsylvania)*

almost a certainty. Some said that the railroad would link up with the Northern Pacific at Loomiston (present-day Loomis), thus shortening the route from the sound to St. Paul by 250 miles.

By mid-1892, some of the new rolling stock had arrived. The cars were custom-built at the Barney and Smith Car Manufacturing Company in Dayton, Ohio, and then transported via rail to Everett. All were equipped with improved

General Manager Finney's private train at Lowell, Washington. The business car is lettered Missouri, Kansas & Texas. This is not the business car later acquired by the Everett & Monte Cristo Railway but is probably similar. One of the men standing at the left is Finney. *(Everett Public Library Collection, King & Baskerville Photo, #097)*

Gould automatic couplers—a knuckle coupler as opposed to the earlier link-and-pin type. This, said the conductor L. W. Speer, would make coupling cars safer for the trainmen and also save time. It included the latest quick-action airbrake, and the brake beams were made of iron pipe instead of wood. The brake hand wheel was movable and could be folded down into a socket at the end of the car and stay completely out of the way if a plow had to be used.

By early August, the 847-foot tunnel #1 was bored about 450 feet, and completion was expected by October. The recently installed compressor plant was expected to increase the pace of progress along the canyon. Work on the 530-foot tunnel #7 had ceased at one end, and cement sand was being removed from the other end to build embankments along the grade. Farther up the line at the little mining camp of Silverton, a hospital was built for treating sick and injured railroad workers. Grading had been completed from Hartford to tunnel #1, a distance of 13 miles. However, the first shipment of rails, delivered by the ship *Guy C. Goss*, covered only about 6 miles of grade. Meanwhile, crews were putting in a switch at the nailworks dock so that cargo could be unloaded there and delivered over the railroad's own line, thus eliminating the need to pay freight charges over other rail lines.

By September 1, the second ship, the *Anne H. Smith*, was overdue. While rounding Cape Horn, it encountered a fierce storm and had to limp over to the Falkland Islands for repairs. By mid-September, the third ship, the *Abner Coburn*, was also overdue. Ships that had left New York after the *Anne H. Smith* and the *Abner Coburn* had already docked in San Francisco.

A section crew poses with its track gauge and handcar before the eastern portal of tunnel #1, the longest on the line. This end of the tunnel was bored into solid rock, but the other half was dug through loose rock and soil. At least twice in the life of the railroad, the timbers caught fire and caused half of the bore to collapse. The Stillaguamish River is beyond the lower left of the photo. *(Phil Woodhouse Collection)*

The *Guy C. Goss*. The date and location of this photo are not known, but this is what the ship would have looked like when unloading supplies at Everett for the railroad. *(Puget Sound Maritime Historical Society)*

The *Abner Coburn* under full sail. It was the second ship to arrive in Everett carrying rails and other iron for the Everett and Monte Cristo line. A labor dispute delayed the unloading, but the precious rails were soon rushed to the construction camps up the line, allowing the railroad to complete the tracks to the vicinity of tunnel #1 in Robe Canyon. *(Puget Sound Maritime Historical Society)*

The *Abner Coburn* carried 2,000 tons of rails— enough for about 25 miles of track—from Pittsburgh, where the rails were manufactured, by way of New York. Its cargo was to be shipped from Everett over company tracks to Snohomish, thus saving the cost of transportation from Seattle over the Seattle Lake Shore and Eastern tracks. The *Abner Coburn*'s cargo combined with what the *Guy C. Goss* had delivered would cover the distance to tunnel #1 from Hartford. With a smelter under construction at a site near the northern end of the Everett peninsula, the sidetracks to it from the Everett and Monte Cristo being laid, and winter on the way, it was imperative that the rest of the railroad be completed quickly.

At Monte Cristo, plans were underway for the long aerial tramways from the mines to the concentrator. The concentrating mill would reduce raw sulfide-bearing ore to a consistency of very fine sand and separate the waste rock from the minerals. The minerals would then be loaded into railroad cars and shipped to the

Monte Cristo in about 1896. The concentrator is the large structure on the left. *(Enid Nordlund Collection, originally in U.S.G.S. Ore Deposits of Monte Cristo, 22nd Annual Report, 1900-1901)*

smelter, where they would be further refined. The waste rock would be dumped at the concentrator, thus saving the expense of shipping large amounts of waste over the rails and paying the smelter fees for concentrating it. The equipment would be brought in via the rails. While the rails were still on the *Abner Coburn*, all that could be done was grading of the right-of-way, work on the tunnels, and ballasting of the roadbed.

Work on tunnel #1 pro-gressed at a rate of 6 feet per day on the west end and 3 feet per day on the east end. Only 200 feet of blasting and tunneling was left to connect the two ends. But scarcity of men continued to plague the project. The *Everett Herald* reported that at tunnel #7 (the "Mud Tunnel"), "a perfect Niagara of mud and water" had made work so unpleasant and dangerous that men were turn-ing down offers of double and even triple wages to work there. Nowhere in the tunnel had they encountered solid rock. The final blow came on the day when the tunnel foreman, walking toward the breast (face) of the tunnel, noticed a hissing sound. Not wanting to alarm the men, and considering that it was near lunchtime anyway, he ordered the workers out. The foreman went in to investigate but felt a slight movement of the earth. Knowing that this meant insta-bility in the tunnel and a prob-able cave-in, he turned and ran for the mouth of the tunnel, some 230 feet away. As he ran, the hissing increased, as did his pace. Upon reaching the portal, he did not attempt to outrun the now deafening roar behind him, but instead turned and clawed his way up the bank as tons of mud, rock, sand, and gravel shot out of the opening.

The rock above tunnel #4 was the nemesis of section hands and laborers on the line. Rockslides were frequent and sometimes deadly. Here, a large crew clears a slide. The crews relied on tools such as shovels, picks, and handcars. Fed up with the rockslide problem, the Northern Pacific closed the line in the summer of 1911 and blew the top off the tunnel, converting it into an open cut. *(Enid Nordlund Collection)*

The workers had unknowingly struck a large pocket of quicksand under pressure, and this quicksand escaping into the tunnel had made the hissing sound. After that incident, the workers refused to go back into the tunnel for any wage. The contractor considered bringing in a crew of 50 Negro miners from the Franklin and Newcastle coal mines to dig a large open cut though the hill, but this idea never materialized, and a "shoo-fly" was built around the hill above the river.

A popular local story told of seven Chinese men and a steam locomotive that were buried in the tunnel when it collapsed. However, no one of Chinese origin ever worked on the construction of the line. Also, steam locomotives were never run into unfinished tunnels because their fires would have quickly consumed the oxygen in the tunnel and the exhaust would have made the air toxic. Whenever steam locomotives delivered goods to a new tunnel, the materials were placed on a flatcar, with other cars between it and the locomotive to allow the locomotive to remain outside the bore when the car with the goods reached the tunnel face. Another reason that the story could not have been true is that there were no rails in place anywhere near tunnel #7 when it collapsed.

By October, word came that the *Abner Coburn* had been sighted and contacted 1,000 miles northwest of Cape Horn on August 17. But there was still no sign of the *Anne H. Smith*. On November 3, the *Abner Coburn* arrived in Everett. The journey had taken 174

Chinese Labor

The stories about Chinese laborers working on the Everett and Monte Cristo line are all myths. During that time, anti-Chinese sentiment was widespread and zealous throughout the western United States. In the mid-1800s, large numbers of Chinese men had come to the United States from southern China to escape the political unrest. Their goal was to earn money to send home to their families and eventually return to China to buy land. The Chinese found ample work building railroads such as the Central Pacific and in the mines of California and other locations in the West.

The mid- to late 1800s also saw a huge influx of unskilled labor from Europe. Unlike the Chinese, the Europeans typically brought their families and had every intention of becoming Americans. They, too, found work on the railroads, as well as in the forests, farms, mines, and other places where unskilled labor was in demand. Much of the Everett and Monte Cristo was built by Italian immigrants.

The economic depressions in the late 1800s caused huge drops in the demand for labor. The resulting competition between Chinese and European laborers for jobs led also to strong anti-Chinese sentiment. Politicians eagerly exploited the antipathy between the Chinese and the Europeans and spread the belief that Chinese were taking jobs away from European Americans by accepting lower wages and a lower standard of living. Ultimately, the fervor against the "Yellow Peril" exploded throughout the west in riots and killings.

In 1882, Congress passed the Chinese Exclusion Act, which prohibited further immigration by Chinese laborers. Interestingly, this sentiment did not apply to the fairly large number of Japanese nationals then living in the United States, many of whom lived and worked in areas that prohibited Chinese from establishing residence, including Snohomish County. The 1900 census of the town of Monte Cristo lists a number of Japanese residents. Furthermore, several bunkhouses along the Everett and Monte Cristo line housed Japanese section crews.

The anti-Chinese sentiment prevailed well into the 20th century. The Chinese Exclusion Act was not formally repealed until 1943, when the United States became allied with China against the Japanese in World War II and anti-Asian sentiment turned against the Japanese after the bombing of Pearl Harbor.

days from New York to Port Townsend. Captain J. C. Gilmore recounted a long, battering journey around the Horn in which the ship had lost one or two sails. The railroad finally got its 1,684 rails (weighing 2,500 tons), 5,890 fishplates, 120 kegs of bolts and nuts, and 890 kegs of spikes.

In the canyon, four tunnels were completed and the remaining two were nearly completed. On October 21, the first excursion train over the new railroad line left Everett for Snohomish, carrying Democrats and delegates for the upcoming November elections and their wives to a rally.

In late 1892, the *Anne H. Smith* finally delivered its cargo of railroad hardware, thus clearing the final obstacle to completion of the railroad. At Monte Cristo, the Wilmans brothers and the Colby-Hoyt Syndicate waited to ship tramway parts over the line, while the United Concentration Company was eager to move heavy equipment for its big concentrating mill to the mill site. At Silverton, the 45 Mining Company was planning a long-aerial tramway from its mines at the headwaters of Williamson Creek (in the Sultan Basin to the south) over Marble Pass to meet the railroad just below Silverton. Every major move along the line depended on the completion of the railroad.

The "Hundred-Year Storm"

The lofty peaks around Silverton were already covered with fresh snow in November 1892, and the snowpack was growing each night. But on November 16, Mother Nature's mood changed. The temperature rose rapidly, the wind began to blow out of the southwest, and for several days a fierce rainstorm raged. Both the Great Northern and Everett and Monte Cristo lines in the Snohomish Valley were under water in places. The Snohomish River ran 20 feet above the low-water mark—the highest it had been since 1872. The entire lower half of Snohomish City was flooded. The Great Northern bridge at Snohomish was threatened, and every wagon bridge on the Everett and Monte Cristo tote road between Granite Falls and Silverton was washed away. In the canyon, water ran through tunnel #6, filling it with logs and debris. Cribbing and ballasting were washed away almost the entire length of the roadbed. One man drowned—a fellow named George Meader.

The *Engineering News* of October 5, 1893, said that in 1892 "great boulders were carried down and tossed about the canyon, striking against one another and the sides of the canyon grinding, grating, and clashing with a noise almost deafening."

It seemed that the old timers were right about the weather, but not as far as the syndicate was concerned. The businessmen believed that this was a freak "100-year storm," and they ordered repairs along the line and regrading along the same right-of-way.

The Everett and Monte Cristo was interested in building a cutoff or shortcut from Hartford to Everett. It would make for a shorter route between the points and would eliminate the need to lease trackage rights from other railroads (notably the Seattle Lake Shore and Eastern). The company made surveys for two plans: a line from Everett to Lake Stevens and a line to meet the Great Northern (Seattle and Montana Railroad) near Marysville and connect with the Stillaguamish section at or near Hartford. Neither plan was undertaken.

By early December, the tracklaying contractors, Henry and Balch, had resumed work following the post-storm cleanup, and they completed their work by Christmas. Above the canyon, most of the contractors had escaped serious damage from the November storm.

Miller and Waky, who had a contract to grade 2½ miles above Silverton, had completed their work and left, while the contractor McGee had only a few weeks of work left below Silverton. At the ill-fated tunnel #7, contractor John Earl was preparing to make the tunnel into an open cut 104 feet deep.

This photo from the June 1902 issue of *Coast Magazine* shows locomotive #4, an American type (4-4-0), which the Everett and Monte Cristo purchased secondhand from the Union Pacific Railroad and assigned to pull many of the passenger trains. The wooden cribbing that often washed away when the Stillaguamish River rose and poured through tunnel #6 (from which the train is emerging), was encased in concrete from Robe to the tunnel. The rails were also set in concrete through the tunnel, with the cribbing encasement continuing halfway to tunnel #5. *(Coast Magazine)*

Looking up the Snohomish River as a railroad Howe truss turn bridge is opened to allow a river steamboat to pass. This was probably the Everett and Monte Cristo bridge near Lowell, which was originally built by the 3S Railway. *(Enid Nordlund Collection)*

A November 1911 flood in Lowell. The depot was originally built by the Everett and Monte Cristo and then rebuilt after it was destroyed by fire in 1898. By 1911 it belonged to the Northern Pacific. The elevated tracks to the left of the depot belonged to the Everett-Snohomish Interurban. *(Warren Wing Collection, Brady photo)*

Locomotive #3 backs a consist of passenger cars in Robe Canyon between tunnel #5 (shown) and tunnel #4 (just below the photographer). The workmen were probably putting timber bracing inside tunnel #4. This photo was probably taken by official photographer Herman Siewart in 1893, before the line was completed past Robe. There was not yet any method of turning the locomotive around, so it pushed the cars up the tracks from Granite Falls and pulled them back down. *(Walt Meglassen Collection)*

Tunnel #5, 95 feet long and the shortest on the line, in Robe Canyon in 1894. In the distance is tunnel #4, with a passenger train about to enter. This train was likely pulled by locomotive #3, which was usually assigned to pull the varnish. After 1900, locomotive #99 (formerly #4) was often used to pull the passenger trains. *(Frank LaRoche photo)*

3

The Railroad's Early Years

O n November 30, 1892, three first-class passenger coaches and two combination mail, express, and baggage cars arrived in Everett over the Northern Pacific Railway. Built in Dayton, Ohio, by Barney and Smith Car Manufacturing Company, they were among the handsomest cars seen in the Northwest. The interior wood, including the seats, was of quartersawn oak, while the roof had a lighter-than-usual veneer finish. The framework was entirely of fir. All of the cars had cast steel wheels and were fitted with air brakes. The mail and baggage cars were said to have all the modern conveniences.

In January 1893, Everett and Monte Cristo General Manager F. N. Finney arrived in Everett in a special car belonging to the Wisconsin Central Railroad to inspect the new line. Accompanying him were three other men, including his son, John C. Finney. After the excursion, which reached only to the first crossing of the Stillaguamish River just below the canyon, Finney confidently predicted that the entire line would be completed by May 1. He also announced that Superintendent Allen of the Everett and Monte Cristo would go east with him and take the position of general superintendent with an "important eastern line." Chief Engineer Fisher, who had been in charge of the construction, would succeed him as superintendent.

By early February 1893, despite unfavorable weather, work on the bridge at the first crossing of the Stillaguamish River was finished and the second, at Rotary, was nearly completed as well. The 3S portion of the railroad from Everett to Snohomish had also been completed, and trains were running between the two towns.

The wet, miserable weather earlier in the winter had played havoc with the tunnel builders on both the Everett and Monte Cristo and Great Northern lines. The Great Northern actually postponed work on the big tunnel under Everett until the rains stopped and

A small portion of an 1894 photo of Monte Cristo. The original negative is 18 inches high by 36 inches wide. Locomotive #3 of the Everett and Monte Cristo Railway hides behind a crummy (work car) while waiting to pull the daily passenger train to Everett. The building behind the crummy is the railway station, which was originally a sawmill erected by the mining companies to supply timber to their mines. *(Frank LaRoche photo)*

the ground dried sufficiently to permit excavation and brickwork. By mid-February, only $3^1/_2$ feet of snow remained at Silverton, and the rails were laid through the canyon to the second crossing.

In Everett, work on ballasting the tracks north from Lowell and around the north end of the peninsula commenced. A new 32-by-44-foot station on Pacific Avenue in Everett was close to completion. The building's roof projected well over the platform, and coal bins were to be placed farther north on the tracks. Passenger trains began running four times daily between Everett and Snohomish on April 10, and by the end of April the trains also ran from Hartford to the end of the line at the far end of the canyon. Visitors to the mining camps at Silverton and Monte Cristo could ride the train over the 3S portion from Everett to Snohomish. The train would then switch to the Seattle Lake Shore and Eastern tracks and connect back to the Everett and Monte Cristo at Hartford on Mondays, Wednesdays, and Fridays. This lessened the agony of overland travel on horseback or stage by 20 miles.

The *Everett Herald* described a party of prominent New Yorkers who traveled to "the front" by this route in May 1893. "After the train left the Pilchuck Valley and rounded the first foothills into the Stillaguamish Valley," the article said, "the scenery at once began to attract attention, and when the train finally entered the tortuous canyon the party went wild with enthusiasm. Looking at the turbulent waters tumbling over the rocks, whirling in graceful eddies and crowding through narrow defiles with cascades and waterfalls bursting into view from the wooded depths, while the train pursues its winding way toward the summit, penetrating tunnels and skirting the river bank, the picture was one of wild grandeur and beauty which is said to rival any similar scenery on the continent."

The Everett depot of the Northern Pacific Railway, which replaced the original Everett and Monte Cristo depot that had been approximately where the shed labeled "D" is shown in the photo. Near "C" were the Everett engine house and car repair shops. Chestnut Street, leading northward, is just beyond the corner of the building. *(Warren Wing Collection)*

In the mountains, miners and merchants eagerly awaited the spring thaw that would permit development to continue unhindered. On May 10, Henry Pennycock, who was in charge of one camp on the Everett and Monte Cristo line 7 miles from Monte Cristo, reported a total snowfall for the winter of 36$\frac{1}{2}$ feet, with 7 feet remaining at the camp and 3$\frac{1}{2}$ feet at Silverton. The snowfall had begun on January 19, when it was 22 degrees below zero, and continued until 9 feet had accumulated. Strangely, hardly any snow fell on the Sauk side of the divide despite the heavy snow on the Stillaguamish side. Pennycock also reported that goods were being hauled to the Silverton area on sleighs.

On June 29, 1893, the last spike was driven into the tracks at Silverton. A new sawmill was already cranking out lumber for buildings and construction projects in and around the area, and stores and businesses were going up all over the town. Surveying parties worked on completing the town plat. The roadbed was nearly complete and free of snow, and workers were laying about 3,000 feet of track per day toward Monte Cristo. They hoped to be done by the end of July. The tote road was free of snow and repaired, so supplies and men could move along it to Monte Cristo and

The Lowell depot of the Northern Pacific Railway in May 1928. The original Everett and Monte Cristo depot, built on the same site, burned to the ground in 1898. In the early days, the town of Lowell was home to many workers and their families. Today, Lowell is a historic district within the city of Everett. *(Dan Cozine Collection)*

The Lowell depot, looking north. The track in front of the depot was built by the Everett and Monte Cristo and is shown here in 1928 when it belonged to the Northern Pacific. Until the Everett tunnel was built in 1900, the Seattle & Montana Railway (a subsidiary of the Great Northern) leased the right to use this track from the Everett and Monte Cristo. After the tunnel was built, the Great Northern built the single track visible at the left. The trestle labeled "B" belonged to the Chicago, Milwaukee, St. Paul & Pacific Railroad and was built in 1911. *(Dan Cozine Collection)*

railroad construction camps with ease. The activity came to a halt that evening as the townspeople celebrated the railroad's arrival with cheers and giant powder blasts that could be heard up and down the valleys.

By mid-July, the first construction train entered Silverton, and daily passenger service from Everett to Silverton began soon after. The train left Everett about 9:30 a.m. for Snohomish, traveled over the Seattle Lake Shore and Eastern tracks to Hartford, and then over its own tracks to Silverton. The return trip gave passengers a good look at Everett before they made connections with northbound or southbound trains or with steamers to other points. Tracklayers were just 4 or 5 miles east of Silverton and pushing steadily forward, although rain slowed their progress.

The nationwide financial crisis—the Panic of 1893—left the Seattle Lake Shore and Eastern bankrupt, and the receiver for the line refused to allow Everett and Monte Cristo trains over Seattle Lake Shore and Eastern tracks. Rumors were revived that the cutoff between Everett and Hartford would soon be built so that the trains would have a way to get from Everett to Hartford without having to travel through Snohomish.

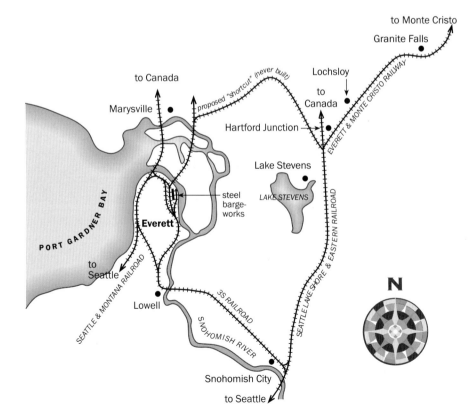

The railroads in the Everett area in 1893. The Seattle & Montana Railway, a subsidiary of the Great Northern, was absorbed by the Great Northern in 1907. The Seattle Lake Shore and Eastern went bankrupt and was purchased by the Seattle & International Railway, a subsidiary of the Northern Pacific. The S&I was absorbed by the Northern Pacific in 1901. The Snohomish, Skykomish, and Spokane Railway and Transportation Company (3S) was built in 1892 but never operated under its original name.

THE "BIG FOUR"
FROM E.&M.C. TRACK.

Big Four Mountain, with the rail line in the foreground, sometime between 1894 and 1897. This photo was probably taken by Herman Siewart, the official photographer of the railway; it is typical of his work. Notice the rail cycle in the foreground and the two men fishing in the Stillaguamish River. Big Four Mountain was named not for the number of its peaks but for the big number "4" that forms in its snowfields when viewed from high up near the mines at Monte Cristo. *(Everett Public Library Collection)*

Silverton in winter. The railroad ran on the other (north) side of the Stillaguamish River. A steel truss bridge carried road and foot traffic across the river. Silverton, originally called Camp Independence, predated Monte Cristo by a few years and was the center of mining for copper and silver, with gold as a secondary metal. When the Everett and Monte Cristo Railway was run down the Stillaguamish River, it made Silverton one of its stops. *(Enid Nordlund Collection)*

Silverton

When gold, silver, and copper ore was discovered in the area 22 miles east of Granite Falls around 1890, a stampede of fortune seekers descended and a small mining camp sprang up on the only level spot in the valley for miles. The camp was originally called Camp Independence, but the name was soon changed to Silverton when the postal service refused to deliver mail to the area, fearing confusion with Independence, Oregon.

An early picture of Camp Independence, later renamed Silverton. Silverton benefited immensely from the Everett and Monte Cristo Railway tracks being built through the town in 1893. Copper was the primary metal sought in the nearby mountains. While a fair amount of mineral was wrested from the local veins, no big strike was ever made. *(Marysville Historical Society, R. Teeple photo)*

New mines and prospects were filed almost daily with names such as Independence, Anacortes, Bonanza Queen, Hoodoo, 45, and Little Chief gaining fame throughout the mining world.

By 1893, the town boasted a number of hotels, restaurants, saloons, a church and school, barber shop, cigar shop, livery stables, and other mining-related businesses, as well as a railroad depot.

The commerce in the community was dependent on the many mines and prospect holes in the area, and the Everett and Monte Cristo Railway enticed many enterprises into the area. With the popular tourist trains passing through town, the town became a destination resort.

Today, a handful of residents call Silverton home and a few dozen summer cottages dot the valley.

Silverton in the 1890s. The photo shows the kinds of commerce that did well in this environment: food, lodging, and supplies. Note the oil lamps on the sidewalks, which were probably installed for saloon patrons, not as a public safety feature. *(Marysville Historical Society, R. Teeple photo)*

Bridge #57 on the Monte Cristo line, about 3 miles below the town of Monte Cristo. Silvertip Peak looms on the skyline. This area is now known as Twin Bridges, after the twin auto bridges that cross the Sauk River at this point. *(Enid Nordlund Collection)*

The view that a rider on the pilot beam of a locomotive would have had as the train approached Monte Cristo from the switchback area about a half-mile below the end of the line. The forest had been decimated by logging and fires. Wilmans Peak rises to the left in the distance, while Columbia Peak graces the skyline at the rear of '76 Gulch in the distant right. Just through the trees on the far right is Toad Mountain, directly above the town. *(Everett Public Library Collection, Gerwys Michal donation)*

Monte Cristo with '76 Gulch behind it. Prospector's Peak is on the right, and Columbia Peak is in the center. A locomotive of the Everett and Monte Cristo Railway—probably locomotive #3—is ready to pull the daily passenger train to Everett. The building on the far left is the United Concentration Company's concentrator. The railway's water tower and engine house are on the far right. *(Granite Falls Historical Society Collection)*

On August 8, 1893, the tracklayers were within a mile of Monte Cristo, working on the switchback right before the town. By August 14, the tracks reached town, and the ballasting was completed shortly thereafter. Trains began running between Everett and Summit (Barlow Pass) three days a week. The route used the Seattle Lake Shore and Eastern tracks from Snohomish to Hartford, once again putting to sleep plans for a cutoff route between Everett and Hartford. (The Seattle Lake Shore and Eastern receivers had come to an agreement with the Everett and Monte Cristo.)

By late August, trains could run all the way to Monte Cristo. In September, a Sunday excursion train began running from Everett to Monte Cristo. Passengers left Everett at 7:30 a.m. and arrived at Monte Cristo at 11:30 a.m.; they left Monte Cristo at 3:30 p.m. and arrived in Everett at 7:30 p.m. Visitors had time to visit the noted mining camp and view the magnificent scenery of the Stillaguamish Canyon and valley. The fare was $2.50 for the round trip.

Another small portion of a photo of Monte Cristo taken in 1894 by Frank LaRoche. (See also page 36.) The Everett and Monte Cristo main line enters the town on the far right. The trestle in the center is the concentrator spur. The old stables and boarding house are on the far left, with the bulk of the United Concentration Company's mill beyond. Dumas Street, the town's main thoroughfare, is to the right of center. The Rialto Hotel (which burned in 1895) is the first building on the left of Dumas, while just above and across the street on the right is the Pioneer Market. *(Phil Woodhouse Collection, Frank LaRoche photo)*

On September 20, General Manager John T. McBride and the general contractor, Henry and Balch, made the final examination of the line. Monday-through-Saturday rail service began that month. On October 19, McBride announced that a station would be established at Snohomish and located just north of the wye that connected the 3S line to the Seattle Lake Shore and Eastern tracks.

With the line in service, much of the badly needed machinery and supplies began to arrive in Monte Cristo, Silverton, and the other camps along the line. The prospectors, miners, and other explorers who previously had to struggle into the mines and claims in the mountains could now travel in comfort, making the trip in a single day.

Another Fierce Winter

With winter approaching, the railroad ordered a large rotary snowplow to keep the mountain tracks clear. It was of the Leslie pattern and was built by a firm in Paterson, New Jersey. By early November, it became clear that the previous winter's weather was no fluke. Chinook winds and heavy rains once again combined to melt snow in the mountains and raise river levels to flood stage. In the Snohomish Valley, E. D. Smith's mill was forced to shut down. A logjam at the Lowell Bridge stopped steamboat traffic for three days. The Snohomish River was running 14 feet above the low-water mark. On the South Fork of the Stillaguamish River, the wagon bridge at Bogardus was carried downstream for 5 miles and smashed to pieces on the railroad bridge at Rotary, the second crossing. At Robe, the kitchen of Truitt K. Robe's house was washed down the river. Trains were delayed on the eastern end of the road when two small washouts occurred between the tunnels in the canyon and some fill gave way near Silverton. At Monte Cristo, water flooded the yard and turntable but did no serious damage. Repairs were soon made and train service resumed over the road.

Later that month, snow began to fall in the mountains. By December 11, 20 inches were on the ground at Monte Cristo. That day, rail service to the

At the town of Robe, a group of dandies rides the pilot beam of locomotive #3 up to Monte Cristo. The locomotive was a Ten Wheeler 4-6-0 built in 1893 in Paterson, New Jersey, by the Cooke Locomotive Works. It burned coal and sported an acetylene headlamp, which was common in its day. The identities of the men are unknown, but they might have been officers who helped build the line and the mining ventures at Monte Cristo. Notice the engineer waiting to get under way while the brakeman lubricates the side rods. *(Enid Nordlund Collection; photographer unknown, but possibly Herman Siewart)*

mountain village was reduced to three trains per week for the rest of the winter. The railroad's new snowplow left New Jersey on December 13, 1893. It attracted much attention as it crossed the nation because it was the most modern plow available. It was the size of a large boxcar and was painted and varnished in a rich brown with "E. & M.C. Ry. No.1" painted on the side. In the front, rotary knives cut the snow, boring through it and flinging it well off to the side of the tracks. For clearing track along hillsides, the snow could be directed to either side of the tracks, blowing it onto the downward side. Under the plow were "pickers and flangers" to clear ice from the rails. The plow's machinery was driven by a stationary steam engine in the car, while the car itself was pushed forward by a locomotive.

Large banners on each side of the cab proclaimed Everett as "the greatest three-year-old city in the west." The banners gave the population of Everett in 1890 as 50, and in 1893 as 6,000. In charge of the plow was Henry Plummer of the Everett and Monte Cristo's engineering department. Accompanying him on the trip west were one or two mechanics from the machineworks where it was built. With General Manager McBride on

A Leslie-pattern rotary snowplow, the pride of the line, removes the stubborn winter snow from the tracks in the mid-1890s. This plow, resembling a boxcar with a large rotor on the front, had its own boiler and steam engine. As the locomotive drove the plow forward, the spinning rotor's cast-iron knives cut into the snow and flung it off to the side in one motion. *(Phil Woodhouse Collection, Edward L. Meyer photo)*

While the big Leslie-pattern rotary plows could remove great depths of snow from the mountain line, they were no match for the many trees and rocks in the avalanche debris that often covered the tracks. A large crew had to precede the plow, probing the snow with long steel rods to determine whether it was safe to run the plow into the mass. If they missed a large rock, one or more of the iron knives that radiated from the center of the plow could be torn free and launched into the air with the snow. The plow would have to be repaired before it could resume work. *(Phil Woodhouse Collection, David B. Ewing photo)*

board, the plow performed its duties without a problem all the way to Monte Cristo. It ran through snow 4 feet deep, some of it well packed and icy, and hurled it 100 feet or more over the telegraph lines and poles. In addition to the new plow, the railroad planned to keep engine #1, which was equipped with a snowplow at each end and also had flangers, at Monte Cristo all winter, along with a full crew of men.

On January 29, 1894, the plow was called upon again when the train pulled by locomotive #1, consisting of a baggage car and two cars of lumber, arrived at Silverton. A large slide 7 to 12 feet deep and 120 feet long covered the tracks at the summit (Barlow Pass). The crew fired up the plow, which was parked on a sidetrack at Silverton, and coupled it to the front of the train. At the slide, the crew probed the snow for large rocks and trees using long steel rods, and then the plow pushed through the snowdrift with ease. The train arrived at Monte Cristo just 12 minutes behind schedule, and some of that delay was actually due to extra freight.

The total snowfall at Monte Cristo was 17 feet 8$\frac{1}{2}$ inches by February 1. Most of it melted, however, leaving 35 inches on the level. Because of the interruption of rail service between Everett and Snohomish during the previous two years, plans were made to raise the tracks 2$\frac{1}{2}$ feet between Everett and Lowell, with work beginning in March.

On February 15 and 16, the new concentrating mill at Monte Cristo was completed. The boilers were fired up and the entire plant tested. Everything ran like clockwork and it was turned over to the United Concentration Company, which was to operate it. This meant that soon large amounts of concentrates would be ready to be hauled over the line.

(following page) Monte Cristo in the 1890s. This photo captures a feature usually missed by photographers of the time. On the far right, beyond the jumble of buildings, is the three-door engine house for the Everett and Monte Cristo Railway, which could service two locomotives at once. The center and left-hand doors led to the engine stalls, while the right-hand door was probably used by wagon traffic. (Smoke stains are visible above the center and left door, but not above the right door.) The builders of the railroad, who were easterners, miscalculated the mountain weather in Washington. The first few harsh winters convinced them that repairing and servicing cast-iron and steel locomotives in an unheated engine house was impossible. Within a few years, they built a new engine house in Everett at Pacific and Chestnut near the station. *(Phil Woodhouse Collection, Edward L. Meyer photo)*

Wheezing smoke and steam from every joint, an Everett and Monte Cristo loco-motive rams a snowplow (located at the front of the flatcar) up the line around the turn of the century. Snow on the upper portion of the line was a constant winter threat. It reached depths of up to 15 feet on level ground and 50 feet on the ava-lanche tracks that crossed the line in several places. *(Enid Nordlund Collection)*

The need to keep the line open all winter became even greater. In February, 10 feet 5¹/₂ inches of snow fell at Monte Cristo, bringing the total for the winter to 29 feet 5 inches. The new plow handled the job of re-moval quite well. On the last Monday in March, the plow cleared 585 feet of snowslides, and although the snow was 12 to 30 feet deep in places, it fin-ished the job in 4 hours.

Preparing for Prosperity

Granite Falls, one of the major communities along the Everett and Monte Cristo line, was without a formal depot. A de-pot was a status symbol for a town, and being located along a railroad and not having a depot made the town seem like a mere spit in the wind. One hundred and sixty residents of this lumber, farming, ranching, and mining town of several hundred presented a petition to the railroad asking for a depot at the platform where trains had stopped in the past. In re-turn, the petitioners promised to back the Colby-Hoyt Syndicate's drive to have the county seat moved from Snohomish to Everett. (The syn-dicate had major investments in Everett, so moving the county seat there would make business much easier to conduct.) By July 1894, trains were stopping at a new, two-story depot at Granite Falls.

The line began enjoying a brisk shingle-hauling business, and the Northern Pacific furnished a generous supply of cars to meet the demand. Several new shingle mills popped up along the line. The country as a whole was beginning to work its way out of the depression, but most of the mines at Monte Cristo had not started operation because of snow and the need for tramway repairs.

The rolling stock of the railroad was in first-class shape, and all four locomotives had been overhauled and looked as good as new. The passenger cars were also in top condition. The roadbed was said to be so smooth that a passenger could hold a glass of water without risking a spill.

The United Concentration Company's mill at Monte Cristo in the mid-1890s, shortly after the mill began operating. Smoke pouring from the stack shows that the fire was lit and the boiler was providing steam to power the 200-horse-power Corliss steam engine, which powered not only the mill but two DC electric dynamos that lit the mill and the upper end of town with incandescent lights. The dynamos also lit the interior of the covered surface tramway along which mules hauled raw ore from the aerial tramway collector station. The surface tram is the long structure extending from the far side of the concentrator off the photo to the left. To the left of the smokestack is the lower aerial tramway terminal and collector station for the Comet Mine, located 2,700 feet of elevation above the site on the flank of Wilmans Peak. *(Phil Woodhouse Collection, Herman Siewart photo)*

A postcard-type photo of the United Concentration Company's concentrator mill at Monte Cristo in the winter. The ridge of trees in the background defines Mystery Hill, where many of the producing mines were located. The slopes of Cadet Peak rise beyond. The presence of the railway cars to the left—all of them boxcars—indicates that this photo was taken during operation of the mill, between 1894 and 1907. Almost all of the concentrated ore shipped from Monte Cristo to the smelter in Everett was hand-shoveled into piles on the floor of boxcars and hauled down the line. *(Enid Nordlund Collection)*

Summer excursions became popular with tourists, businessmen, and politicians. They took one-day trips from Everett to Monte Cristo, where a few hours were allotted for sightseeing and hiking. Some trains carried 600 or more sightseers. Sometimes a brass band provided entertainment on the open cars. One train was so heavily loaded that two locomotives hauled it up the tracks, one in the front and one in the rear.

In early September of 1894, the Everett and Monte Cristo signed a contract with the Stetson and Post Mill and the Cyphers and Stimson logging company in which the railroad agreed to build a 1,000-foot-long log dump on the bank of the Snohomish River north of the city. The timber companies owned a great deal of timber between Hartford and Granite Falls. This

Another view of the mill at Monte Cristo in 1900. The mill operated from 1894 until 1897, from 1900 until 1903, and again in 1907. Its operations were dictated by accessibility to the railroad and the fortunes of the mining companies. During the savage winter of 1910, the mill's roof collapsed under the weight of the snow, never to be rebuilt. In its heyday, the mill could handle 300 tons of ore per day, concentrating the pay dirt by about 3 or 4 to 1, which reduced shipping costs on the railroad. *(Western History Research Center, University of Wyoming; Josiah E. Spurr photo)*

This unusual photo, which was taken sometime between 1894 and 1910, shows the United Concentration Company's mill from just above Glacier Street in Monte Cristo. The spur line that accessed the concentrator curves across Glacier Creek, while the track leading to the office and assay building is on the left. *(Enid Nordlund Collection)*

contract assured the railroad a fair amount of business over the coming years. By mid-September, carloads of concentrates from the Monte Cristo mines and mill were finally being moved down the tracks on the way to the smelter.

On October 8, while a section crew cleared slide debris at tunnel #4, a mass of rock fell on two of the workers. One was pulled out, unconscious, and died an hour

The Granite Falls depot circa 1896. *(Phil Woodhouse Collection)*

For about three years, beginning in 1900, the Monte Cristo line was known as the Monte Cristo Railway and ran from Hartford Junction to Monte Cristo. This June 1902 photo shows locomotive #99, an American 4-4-0 that was newly painted and sported the line's new logo, an interlocked M and C surrounded by the motto "Scenic Line of the Northwest." It sits on the 150-foot Howe truss deckspan bridge across the Stillaguamish. The locomotive pulls a consist of newly painted passenger cars, all a rich brown and bearing the name of the line in gold on their sides. This train carried a group of Grand Army of the Republic veterans from a meeting at Monte Cristo and is shown after emerging from tunnel #1. *(Various collections, Gifford Pinchot photo)*

One of the early schedule and rate tables of the Everett and Monte Cristo Railway. This one took effect on December 1, 1893. The railroad was completed into the town of Monte Cristo on September 6 of that year. A ride from Everett to Monte Cristo, 68.1 miles up the line, cost $3.40, more than a day's wages in those days. The rate for a corpse was one first-class fare, with someone accompanying the body. *(Enid Nordlund Collection)*

later. The other escaped with a broken arm and leg. This was only one of many slides and cave-ins at tunnel #2 and at tunnel #4.

On October 24 1894, a train was to be dispatched to Silverton and Monte Cristo to ferry people to Everett to celebrate the launch of the whaleback steamer *City of Everett*. However, the train encountered a slide blocking the tracks at tunnel #1. The conductor and his assistants crossed the slide on foot and with the aid of a hand-pumped speeder (a rocking beam mechanism that was attached to a crank that rotated the wheels) made their way up the tracks to within 7 miles of Monte Cristo. From there they walked into town in the pouring rain. At the town, they fired up a locomotive with a boxcar attached and brought people down to the slide. From there they crossed the slide on foot and finished the trip on the other train. They returned home the same way that night, arriving before midnight.

The Rockefeller Reorganization

In late June 1894, Frederick T. Gates, personal secretary to John D. Rockefeller, arrived in Everett. Rockefeller's vast empire stretched across the nation, but because of health problems he could not look after his businesses on his own. He entrusted his holdings to Gates. Rumors had reached Rockefeller as the depression of 1893 hit that much of the money he had entrusted to other investors throughout the country had been poorly spent. He sent Gates to investigate and to correct the situation. Gates was a shrewd businessman in his own right. In the Northwest, he immediately went to work sorting out trouble spots.

One major trouble spot was the management of the various Everett and the Monte Cristo companies, which had been set up by the Colby-Hoyt-Hewitt syndicate and were backed primarily by Rockefeller. The corporate officers were largely the same for the following enterprises:

- The Everett Land Company
- The Puget Sound Reduction Company
- The United Concentration Company
- The Everett and Monte Cristo Railway Company
- The Puget Sound Wire Nail and Steel Company
- The paper mill at Lowell
- The Pacific Coast Steel Barge Company
- The brick works

Funds could easily be transferred from one company to another to allow those that were prospering to support those that were faltering. Gates reorganized the companies and appointed himself president of the operations. Gates set each company on its own feet, to thrive or fail on its own merits. This was particularly hard on the mining companies because the mines had not yet begun to produce. The tramways had not been repaired, and the companies had borrowed money to develop the mines, tramways, and mill.

Gates authorized extensive improvements to the Everett and Monte Cristo line, including a 180-foot snowshed just east of Barlow Pass, additional riprapping (large rocks to stabilize embankments), an overhaul and paint job for the snowplow, new sidetracks in Everett, and a substantial engine house—as much as $75,000 in improvements.

Gates realized during his trip that the money in the Northwest was not in mining but in timber. He set in motion events that would eventually divest Rockefeller of all his mining holdings and reinvest the money in timber.

The Everett and Monte Cristo terminated its contract with Postal Telegraph Company in December and entered into a new contract with Western Union Company in Everett. This move gave the railroad direct communications with Seattle and other points without going though the "repeater" at Snohomish. On December 4, the official county election was held, and by a substantial margin Everett was chosen as the new county seat, beating out Snohomish (with help from the residents of Granite Falls, who were enjoying their new depot). Everettites in Monte Cristo celebrated this news with a fusillade of revolver shots.

Work had begun on raising the grade of the tracks from a point below the bargeworks to the city. It then would be continued to Lowell. This was meant to lessen the chances of delays due to floods in the lowlands.

A census of Monte Cristo taken by the *Monte Cristo Mountaineer* newspaper in January 1895 gave the population as 126 men, 31 women, and 40 children. This number probably did not include men at the outlying mines.

Snowslides in the mountains on either side of Monte Cristo were few and far between during the winter of 1894-95, although in late January, winter weather slowed

In 1902, summer excursions on the Everett and Monte Cristo line were popular. At the rear of the right-hand train, flat cars equipped with railings and bench seats were sometimes coupled to the train to give travelers an unfettered view. This scene is at the switchback about $^2/_3$ of a mile below Monte Cristo. Wilmans Peak forms the backdrop. (Coast Magazine, *George W. Kirk photo*)

business and the mines were closed while new equipment was installed at the concentrator. By the end of February 1895, the snow was nearly gone in the mountains east of Everett. With spring in the air, most of the business for the railroad came from the logging camps and shingle mills.

New camps were nearing completion and established camps were making improvements. At Monte Cristo, the long aerial tramways were overhauled in preparation for summer. Triweekly train service from Everett to Monte Cristo began again on May 6. Everything pointed to a prosperous summer, not only for the railroad but for the mines and mills scattered across Snohomish County. The railroad expected to spend $7,000 that summer for the construction of three new sidetracks. Two would be logging spurs 2 miles above Hartford and at Perry Creek above Silverton, and the third would be a spur directly connecting the ore collector bunker above Monte Cristo with the main line, bypassing the concentrator. Six to eight carloads of ore were shipped out of Monte Cristo on every train,

A July Fourth parade in Everett. A model of the whaleback steamer *Wetmore* is on the wagon on the left. Because of the depression, the steamer was the only ship ever built at the steel bargeworks on the Snohomish River. Behind it is a huge timber that was cut at a local mill. The Everett and Monte Cristo Railway had to make special provisions to transport people who lived along the rail line to Everett for the parade. Tunnel #1 had collapsed, and a train was trapped up the line. To get the passengers out, the railway hauled them down the tracks to the blockaded tunnel, where they walked over the precipitous pathway to reach the other side. From there, a second train carried them into town. *(Enid Nordlund Collection)*

One of the major commodities hauled on the railroads in the Everett area was large timber. The Everett and Monte Cristo Railway wound through the virgin forest that stretched from Puget Sound to the slopes of the Cascades. These virgin climax forests had never been cut. Some of the Douglas firs stood over 400 feet high and were over 17 feet in diameter at the 12-foot mark. One tree could provide a load for an entire train, as seen here. The trees were cut by axes and crosscut saws (known appropriately as "misery whips"). *(Phil Woodhouse Collection)*

and the railroad received an application for a sidetrack at Deer Creek that would serve the mines of this promising valley, in particular the big Bonanza Queen Mine and the St. Louis Jackson Mines.

In the lowlands, light-duty rails were replaced with heavy-duty rails between Everett and Lowell, while the old light rails were moved up the line and used on the new spurs. By August 1, stakes had been driven into the ground for the new engine house about 200 yards north of the Everett depot. The project included a low-level trestle for tracks north of the building. That month, 100 cars of shingles from 11 camps were transported over the line, making it the heaviest shingle-hauling month in the short history of the railroad.

More of Nature's Wrath

On September 3, 1895, the first snowstorm of the season hit Monte Cristo, but the pioneers in the area predicted a mild winter and the popular excursion trains to Monte Cristo were expected to run all season. The mines at Monte Cristo were also expected to continue work through the winter, thus assuring a profitable season. By November, the engine house in Everett was complete and work was in progress on the replacement roundhouse at Monte Cristo. (The original roundhouse at Monte Cristo was unsuitable for the bitter and savage winter weather. Once the builders realized their mistake, they built the engine house in Everett.) More sidetracks were laid on the lower side of the present tracks at Monte Cristo, and coal bunkers were planned for that end. Facilities for handling ore from the mines were enlarged.

At Goat Lake, located in the valley just north of Monte Cristo, the mines shut down for the winter. On December 5 and 6, tragedy struck again at tunnel #4 when a large slide blocked the tracks. A section crew was dispatched to clear the line. A lookout's shout from above was too late to save the crew working below as another slide pounded down the mountainside. A 25-year-old worker was killed, the foreman's head was injured, and another man's leg was broken. The accident happened at the same spot where a year earlier a slide had broken another man's leg.

On Christmas morning, a train started for the mountain hamlet in a raging storm. Snow now lay 6 feet deep on the level, and drifts continued to pile much higher in some places. This train was double ended, with a big rotary plow in front. It reached Silverton

A Rebuilt Rail Car

One of several flatcars that were badly burned in a fire at Cyphers and Stimson's mill was taken to the railroad's Everett shop and completely rebuilt (except for the iron frame) under the direction of Master Mechanic Henry Huden. The Sumner Iron Works in Everett made the castings for the wheels. The new sills were made from Douglas fir and were 5-by-5 inches inside and 5-by-3 inches outside. They were 34 feet long and without a blemish. The original cars were from the east. They had sills made of eastern pine and had not been strong enough to withstand the rigors of the logging business. Sixteen of the old sills had broken. The rebuilt car was the pride of the maintenance department, which neatly painted "Everett and Monte Cristo Railway Shops" on the side.

Medium-sized logs are stacked and secured on a rebuilt Everett and Monte Cristo flatcar for their trip to a mill. The railroad provided the only means of transporting such cargo at the turn of the century. *(U.S. Forest Service, Darrington Ranger District)*

The Sumner Iron Works around the turn of the century. This factory produced much of the heavy machinery for the area in the 1890s and 1900s, including boilers, sawmill machinery, mining machinery, steam engines, and water wheels. *(Enid Nordlund Collection)*

The water tower in Silverton in winter. On a steam locomotive, running out of fuel was less of a worry than running out of water. If the water level in the boiler got so low that it uncovered the crown sheet over the firebox, an explosion could blow the locomotive to bits. To prevent this, water towers were spaced at carefully measured intervals along the line. In mountain country, where the locomotives had to work harder, the towers were placed closer together than they were on the flat. *(Phil Woodhouse Collection)*

without much problem, but beyond Silverton trees were down in many places and the tracks were covered with several feet of snow, rendering the big plow almost useless. The weary crew returned the train to Silverton, where they enjoyed their Christmas dinner.

Five gangs of section men began the laborious job of clearing the tracks above Silverton that night, and at 4:30 the next morning the train once again started for Monte Cristo. After a day of hard work removing downed trees from the tracks, the train finally arrived at Monte Cristo at 7:30 p.m., where a jubilant crowd of mountain souls welcomed it. The storm began to abate that day, and after a night and day of rest the train started its return trip to Everett, this time with more laborious clearing work. The rotary plow and caboose were left up the road, while the engine and passenger coach plied their way on down the line, arriving at Everett the next morning. Upon reaching Everett, the train was completely encrusted in snow. The next day's trip was canceled.

By mid-January 1896, the bad weather had abated somewhat, and a force of 20 or more men made repairs to the storm-damaged railroad. A flanger, which ran on compressed air and kept the inside area between the tracks free of ice, was also put in use on the mountain engines. The westbound train from Monte Cristo became snowbound at Barlow Pass on February 11 and a relief train was dispatched with the big rotary snowplow in front to clear the way. A week later, a huge slide 500 feet long and 30 feet deep buried the tracks at

Silverton in December 1922. A steam locomotive was used to open the Hartford Eastern line to this mountain town. The line was often open only to this point because of the avalanches and the snow pack farther up. *(Enid Nordlund Collection)*

A steam locomotive rams its way through the snow into Silverton. With a plow on the locomotive's pilot beam and another on this flatcar, the rails could usually be cleared up the line to Silverton. Beyond that point, however, heavier machinery was often required. The Silverton depot is on the left. *(Phil Woodhouse Collection)*

the switchback near Monte Cristo. The steel knives of the big rotary plow were useless in the hard-packed snow, and a crew had to work with blasting powder and hand tools.

Snow continued to pile up, and by the end of February Everett had 8 inches. At Barlow Pass, the last train of the month from Monte Cristo was stranded by the heavy snow and had to spend the night. The next morning, the snowplow got the train moving again.

Later in the season at Monte Cristo, a huge snowslide parted the big stationary carrying cable on the Mystery Mine tramway. While a crew repaired the tram, another enormous slide roared down from above, sending the men scattering desperately. This avalanche dwarfed the earlier slides, and the snow piled up like miniature mountains in the valley below. It ripped the running cable of the tramway as it passed, shattering the large bullwheel at the mine headhouse. Ore shipments from the Mystery Mine ceased until spring, when a new bullwheel was delivered to the site.

In the town, many buildings were flattened by the heavy snow, including the large boardinghouse of the Monte Cristo Mining Company in the upper town site.

The Floods of 1896

In the Stillaguamish Valley in the spring of 1896, Silverton was preparing for summer exploration work. The Little Chief Mine in the Sultan Basin announced plans to deliver ore to Silverton for shipment over the rails to the smelter in Everett.

Rumors began to circulate that the Everett and Monte Cristo would soon divert the Stillaguamish River into a new channel in an area known as the Sinkhole, thus ending a long and futile battle in which soil settlement and movement constantly displaced and twisted the railroad bed at that spot. In May 1896, the bankrupt Seattle Lake Shore and Eastern Railway was sold to bondholders in Seattle for $1 million over the objections of the parent company, the Northern Pacific.

By early June of 1896, the Pittsburgh Greensburg Mine owners were hurrying construction of their warehouse and rail station at Barlow Pass and repairing and extending the road to its mine at Goat Lake.

By November, snow was 6 to 10 feet deep and rains in the lowlands began to swell the rivers. At Silverton, the talk of the town was the big mineral strike above Deer Lake (Lake Kelcema). Downstream residents began preparing for floods, and ranchers started moving livestock to higher ground. But few, if any, residents expected the two days of warm Chinook winds that quickly melted the vast snowfields, turning the rivers and creeks into foaming torrents. On November 14, the Snohomish River was at the highest level ever recorded. In only a few hours, the river burst over its banks and turned the rich Snohomish Valley into an enormous lake. The lake rose so fast that much livestock was lost. Homes were flooded, and some were carried down the valley. Rail service and all nonfloating transportation came to a complete standstill. The next day, the river was 18 feet above normal.

The stern-wheel steamer *Florence Henry* was dispatched to the flooded valleys to rescue stranded residents. It picked up 22 trapped families the first day and more the next. About 30 homes were lost to the storm's fury. Old-timers said it was much worse than the big flood of 1860, which had held the record. On November 16, temperatures began to drop, giving needed relief to the flood-ravaged lowlands and bringing snow to the mountains.

Despite the savageness of the storm, the railroads suffered only minor ballast washouts because the bridges were closely watched by crews ready to break up floating log-jams with dynamite and gads. Logging camps were not so lucky, however. The rushing waters carried away thousands of logs and de-stroyed or buried a great deal of equipment. The mines and concentrator at Monte Cristo and other points along the line were shut down as workers repaired the tracks.

By month's end, news of the flood began to spread as communication was restored with the rest of the county. Between Snohomish and Monroe, a rancher, his wife, and three children were reportedly drowned while trying to reach higher ground. Near Fiddler's Bluff, upstream from Snohomish, two bolt cutters were forced to climb a large stump after their cabin flooded. They were stranded all night and most of

Crossing the sinkhole just before the station stop of Weigle near Silverton. No matter how many times the railroad workers realigned the trestles, the sliding earth would offset them or cause them to sink. The early engineers were unaware that a 100-foot deep deposit of slippery glacial clay lies under this area. Even today, the Snohomish County road engineers and workers fight this shifting terrain. The road cannot be paved here—it can only be graveled. *(Enid Nordlund Collection)*

the next day until they were rescued by some people in a passing canoe. Near Lowell, some livestock found refuge on the railroad right-of-way that was elevated above the valley floor. At Monte Cristo, the two-story Cleveland and Kline Saloon was swept into the raging Sauk River when it was struck by timbers from the washed-out railroad trestle upstream.

Within days, about 150 miners walked to Snohomish and Everett because provisions were quickly being depleted and the rail service and the mines were not operating. The remaining supplies were saved for the workers and families who stayed behind. To augment the diminishing food supplies, cattle were herded in.

By the second week of December, temperatures again rose, pushed by another Chinook. Again the rivers poured over their banks and ranchers were forced to move to higher ground. The waters came within 2 feet of the record depth in November.

The stern-wheel steamer *Florence Henry,* part of the legendary "mosquito fleet" that plied the waterways of Puget Sound before the railroads and other forms of ground transportation eliminated the need for it. *(Museum of History and Industry)*

This time, the ranchers were a little more prepared, but the railroads were not. Most of the new repair work was lost to washouts. Crews again went to work on the damaged line and more people began the long exodus on foot out of the food-scarce mining and logging camps. Although disastrous, this storm only lasted a couple of days, and by mid-December the track had been repaired as far as Robe at the eastern end of the canyon. By the end of December, the trains were reaching Silverton.

As 1897 began at Monte Cristo, the tracks were still impassable beyond Silverton. With the mines still closed, most of the men were laid off. The company doctor had left some weeks earlier. With his departure, an expectant mother was placed in the care of a handful of remaining miner's wives. While the woman's husband made his way out on foot to procure medicine in Snohomish, it became clear that the little bundle of joy could wait no longer. The women hastily put her on a push car and proceeded down the tracks toward Silverton. The baby was born just a short distance down the track. The group returned to Monte Cristo with mother and baby doing just fine.

A Brighter Outlook

By February 1897, the railroad line was clear and trains were running to Monte Cristo. Despite a deep snowfall in late March, operations along the line began to hum, with big plans for the summer months. With the optimistic outlook for the Silverton and Deer Creek mines, the Everett and Monte Cristo planned a new station and sidetracks at Silverton. In addition, with the increased activity in the Stillaguamish Valley and Deer Creek areas, the railroad began daily rail service to Monte Cristo in late April.

On May 6, 1897, the first carload of lime was shipped to the Everett paper mill over the railroad from the new lime quarry across the river from tunnel #2. The lime was carried across the stream in a large gravity bucket tram and deposited directly into the railroad cars. (This bucket tram was later replaced with a suspension bridge on which large cars similar to miner's ore cars traveled back and forth over the river between the quarry and the railroad tracks.) The lime was found to be of finer quality than lime from the San Juan Island lime quarries, which were considered among the best in the state.

On May 22, the popular excursions to Silverton and Monte Cristo began. Fares were $1 for the round trip to Silverton and $1.25 to Monte Cristo.

So promising were the railroad's prospects that J. B. Crooker and T. W. Foster, vice president and superintendent, respectively, visited Silverton in April to begin planning the

A locomotive under steam waits to make the trip from Monte Cristo to Everett sometime between 1895 and 1897. This is probably locomotive #3, which usually pulled passenger trains. At the far right is the Monte Cristo water tower, and farther to the right is the engine house. The valley at the upper left is '76 Gulch, with Columbia Peak looming above it. *(Granite Falls Historical Society Collection)*

The limestone crushing mill and bins at Cutoff, between Granite Falls and tunnel #1. The lime kilns were also located here. The lime produced at Cutoff was shipped to Lowell for use in paper production and to Everett for use as a flux in the smelting process at the Puget Sound Reduction Company's smelter. *(Enid Nordlund Collection)*

expansion of the railroad's facilities there. They announced plans to construct a new depot and install additional sidetracks to accommodate the increased ore production at the mines. By late April, 1,000 tons of concentrates per week were being sent over the line to the smelter in Everett. At 25 tons per car, that amounted to about 40 cars per week. This brought an average of $1,575 in revenue per week to the railway.

A new hotel was being built at Monte Cristo to cater to the throngs that were riding the rails to the end of the line. The Wilmans brothers were once again operating their Golden Cord Mine and hauling equipment up the railroad and into the mines at a feverish pace. The use of new air drills in the Mystery and Pride of the Mountains mines accelerated the production dramatically. It appeared that prosperity had finally arrived, and that all the delays and disasters of the previous five years had been worth the effort. As summer faded into autumn, early snows began to accumulate on the mountains around Monte Cristo. Despite the prosperity and enthusiasm, nature had other plans for the railroad.

The only known photo of the suspension bridge that crossed the Stillaguamish River and the railroad at the eastern portal of tunnel #2. This was part of a montage of photographs in the October 1907 issue of *Coast Magazine* that depicted the early days in Snohomish County. This bridge was built to carry limestone, which was mined across the river, to the railroad. *(Coast Magazine)*

MONTE CRISTO WN

Ellis
5005

Lime

The lure of precious metals initiated the stampede of prospectors into the Cascades, but other, more mundane minerals were also sought after as the region's industries grew and diversified. One mineral that experienced an early demand was lime, or calcium oxide. Lime is made by heating limestone in a kiln in the absence of air—a process known as "burning." The demand for lime was created by two of the industries that Colby, Hoyt, and Hewitt established as the cornerstones of Everett's economy: the smelter in Everett and the paper mill at Lowell. At the smelter, the lime was used as a flux to more readily smelt the ore and thus extract the metals. At the paper mill, it served as a whitening agent.

Lime could be shipped in from a distance, but at great expense. The first local deposits were discovered right next to the Everett and Monte Cristo right-of-way at Cutoff (between Granite Falls and tunnel #1). To process these deposits, lime kilns were built at Cutoff just a short distance from where the Johnson-Dean spur connected with the main line. The lime was burned near the quarry and then loaded directly onto the railroad cars at the siding next to the kiln.

The deposit was not a large one, however, and the search for other local deposits of limestone uncovered one on the south side of the Stillaguamish River across from tunnel #2. To access this deposit, a suspension bridge was built at the eastern portal of the tunnel and tracks were installed on the bridge to transport small limestone cars from the quarry. Since there was no room in the area to construct lime kilns, the raw limestone was shipped to the existing kilns at Cutoff.

The lime operation on the Monte Cristo line enjoyed a local monopoly on the commodity until enormous deposits were discovered near the town of Clinton on Whidbey Island. A large operation was put into place there and the lime was shipped on barges to points around the Puget Sound. The low price and high quality of the Clinton lime spelled an end to the lime operations along the Monte Cristo line.

One of the two lime kilns and its attendant building at Cutoff. The limestone was mined near this spot just behind the trees. It was crushed and burned and then shipped to Lowell and Everett for use in the production of paper and in the smelting process. *(Enid Nordlund Collection)*

Limestone quarry workers in the South Fork Stillaguamish Valley. *(U.S. Forest Service, Darrington Ranger District)*

(facing page) Monte Cristo in the 1930s viewed from the Boston-American Mine dump. The mine's headquarters/cookhouse is at the lower left. The mine was close to Monte Cristo, while the other major mines were high up on the distant mountains. The only remaining buildings along Dumas Street are the Riddle House at left center and the larger Royal Hotel (Monte Cristo Inn) at right center. The three summits of Cadet Peak pierce the skyline. *(J. Boyd Ellis photo)*

The end of the line at Monte Cristo in the late 1910s or early 1920s, when the line was called the Hartford Eastern. This photo looks up the valley toward the mines. On the right are the remains of the United Concentration Company's mill, and where the tracks stop in the distance is the farthest that the line ever traveled up the valley. The spur leading from the yards at Monte Cristo approaches from the left. The photographer stood on the spur that ran to the office and the assay building near the Monte Cristo town site. High on the hills in the distance are the ruins of the mining buildings. *(Bob Thorsen Collection)*

The Storms of 1897

In November 1897, the wind and rain began in the high country and again the rivers flooded, this time worse than in 1896. Water raged down the canyons, washing out railroad beds and in some places twisting rails into pretzel shapes and destroying bridges and bulkheads. In the lowlands, the rivers once again spread out over the farmland and ranches. The Everett and Monte Cristo reportedly suffered the most damage, with the Great Northern a close second.

The worst damage to the Monte Cristo line was from tunnel #1 at the lower end of the Stillaguamish Canyon all the way to Monte Cristo. In the canyon, the roadbed was almost completely gone. Just above the canyon east of Robe, half of the bridge at Rotary was washed out, and the bridge over the Sauk was destroyed. Parker McKenzie, a Silverton resident who walked out from Silverton after the storm, described the scene for the Seattle *Post-Intelligencer*: "In one place a heavy steel rail is coiled like a spiral spring and stands straight up in the air. Another place a steel rail sticks out over the bank 60 feet or more and right at the end, within 10 inches of the fish plate is broken square off." In other places, the force of the water had bent the rails into the shape of the letter N. At another point, a rail wrapped around a big spruce tree like a giant anaconda. McKenzie also described ties piled like cordwood hundreds of yards downstream. Bridge #27 was lifted off its piers and washed downstream only to land squarely on the piers of bridge #25. McKenzie said it looked like only a few spikes would be needed to make bridge #25 good again.

So much was lost or damaged that some doubted whether the line would be rebuilt at all that season, especially considering that flooding would probably continue for a couple more months. Many wondered whether the line would have to be rerouted around the canyon. This was especially troubling news for the 45 Mining Company, which had just completed a long aerial tramway over Marble Pass to the railroad just west of Silverton. The company was almost ready to start shipping ore over the tramline and the railroad to the smelter in Everett. With no other reasonable egress for the minerals, the mine had to close. Because so much was at stake, the company offered its workforce of 70 men for the repair gangs along the line. Two men who walked out of Monte Cristo after the storm reported that everyone who could was getting out of town.

Destruction or not, supplies still had to be hauled into the nearly inaccessible mining and logging camps, and soon pack trains from tunnel #1 to Silverton were added to move supplies until the railroad could be reopened.

In the area known today as Twin Bridges, the railway ran straight as an arrow up the valley of the Sauk River toward Monte Cristo. Listed as bridge #57 on the Monte Cristo line's engineering drawings, this trestle was an unimposing structure. The scenery, on the other hand, was spectacular. The mountain slope that runs off the photo to the upper left is the side of Silvertip Peak. The fin on its flank has had various names over the years. In this period, it was known as Liberty Peak. *(Enid Nordlund Collection)*

The big rumor was that the railroad would not be rebuilt at all, even though 1897 was a record year for mine production. The 45, Independent, and Goat Lake mines had put many thousands of dollars into their camps and equipment, and the O&B and P&I mines at Monte Cristo were expected to be big producers that year. The owners of the railroad were also the primary shareholders of the major Monte Cristo properties, and they would certainly have much to lose if the road were not reopened. Vice President Crooker of the Everett and Monte Cristo refused to say whether the line would be reopened, but he indicated his personal belief that the Pride of the Mountains Mine at Monte Cristo (owned by the Rockefeller-backed syndicate) was looking "very favorable," which seemed to bode well for the reconstruction of the line.

On December 17, 1897, Frederick T. Gates, the Everett and Monte Cristo president, announced that the railroad would not be rebuilt. He said that it had never paid dividends and that the syndicate mines had not panned out. When other mines along the line were asked by the railroad to agree to higher freight fees in return for restoration of the railroad, the answers ranged from a polite "no" from the 45 Mine owners to "go to hell" from the Penn Mining Company, which decided to build its own roads.

The last remnant of the trestle that carried the railway to Monte Cristo succumbs to nature in the 1940s. *(Enid Nordlund Collection, Ed Nordlund photo)*

A week later, the company announced that the line would immediately be rebuilt as far as tunnel #2 in the canyon to provide transportation to and from the lime quarry just beyond the tunnel. Many hoped that the line would be extended a short distance farther to Robe, where shingles, wood, and bark could be procured for shipment to Puget Sound.

The Kissing Tunnel

The day that Frederick T. Gates announced that the line would not be rebuilt, an article appeared in the Seattle *Post-Intelligencer* titled "Kissing Tunnel: Closing of Monte Cristo Railroad's Famous Attraction":

Now that it is announced that the Everett and Monte Cristo Railroad will not be rebuilt regret will be occasioned that the beautiful scenic route through the Stillaguamish Canyon will be closed to tourists, and nothing will be more missed than the famous kissing tunnel which marked the entrance to the railroad into the canyon. This tunnel is 900 feet long, and from its cool depths flows mineral waters and across its echoing caverns stretches a belt of magnetic iron. This iron is the cause of the wonderful properties of the tunnel. Together with the ozone which the mineral waters of the tunnel produce, and the magnetic current which is occasioned by the passing of the train, passengers are seized with a remarkable osculatory desire. Men have even been known to kiss their wives under the influence of the magnetic current, while callow youths never stopped kissing from the time the train entered the tunnel to the time it emerged from the other side. The lamps were never lighted while going though the tunnel, and the echoes of the puffs of the engine and the noise of the train drowned the loud resounding smacks which would otherwise have shocked elderly ladies and newspaper men. When the tunnel was passed the train again came out in the sunlight, girls would be seen arranging their hair, wives would be blushing pleasantly and old maids sitting in their seats with gentlemen would be noticed to be wearing a joyous smile. The things had long attracted the attention of a naturally observant reporter, but as he was of a timid and retiring nature, and never presumed to sit next to a lady while passing through the tunnel, the true state of affairs remained a mystery. One other incident had aroused his curiosity and that was that E.C. Ferguson, Parker McKenzie and Will Hodgins were constant travelers up and down the road and never missed a chance to occupy a seat with a lady as tunnel #1 was approached. Will Hodgins always went on excursion days and always managed to be the center of the crowd of a half-dozen handsome young ladies just before entering the tunnel. The snap was first given away when an elderly milliner from Seattle overcome by the magnetic current threw herself upon conductor Speer and overwhelmed him with caresses. The road promptly sent her a bill for twenty kisses at five cents each. But the final exposé came when an excursion train packed with rosy-cheeked girls and their lovers stopped square in the middle of the tunnel, giving them full shock of the subtle sweet fluid. The unfortunate men who were alone in the car unfeelingly yelled "break away," "rats," "here comes the light," "I'll tell ya ma," but the force of the current could not be overcome, and since then the tunnel has been known as the kissing tunnel. Nothing will be missed more than this famous tunnel.

Looking up toward Marble Pass. The 2¹/₂-mile aerial tramway of the 45 Mine on the other side in Sultan Basin traveled over the pass. Just beyond the Everett and Monte Cristo tracks was the South Fork of the Stillaguamish River. In at least one instance, this mine and tramway were instrumental in prompting the railroad company to reopen the line after a protracted stoppage of traffic. The mine had continued to operate its silver operation even after the tracks washed out in 1897. This created an enormous stockpile of ore at the mine's Sultan Basin camp. Some of the ore was carried down the Sultan Basin trail by mule and horse, but the railroad was needed. A deal between the mining company and the railroad was at least partly responsible for the railroad's reorganization into the Monte Cristo Railway, which reopened the line in 1900. (Coast Magazine, *June 1902*)

Times of Confusion

In December 1897 and January 1898, the Everett and Monte Cristo Railway explored the idea of running a new route around the canyon. It considered both the north and south sides because both had large stands of timber, the harvesting of which would help defray construction costs. The expense would be greater for the longer distance, but the cost would be passed on to customers because freight rates were based on distance. The southern route would cut through the lime quarry and eliminate the need for two of the Stillaguamish crossings, while the northern route would be considerably longer but would provide access to the promising Whitehorse and Jim Creek areas.

By the end of February 1898, it looked as though the railroad would be pushed north toward the headwaters of Jim Creek from the Canyon Creek area and then along the Oso Valley to the Sauk and south to Monte Cristo. Silverton would have to be accessed from Barlow Pass. This would open up much more fertile farm and timber country than was available in the South Fork valley of the Stillaguamish River.

Meanwhile, workers were repairing the line as far as tunnel #2. They planned to temporarily rebuild the rest of the road and later regrade it permanently to make it safe from floodwaters. In the meantime, survey crews from the 45 Mine laid out a rail route up the Sultan Basin to their mine, which would tap other mines along the way. As spring began, more rumors spread that the Northern Pacific was negotiating the purchase of the Everett and Monte Cristo, or at least the waterfront portion of it.

At Monte Cristo, the Colby-Hoyt syndicate's mines fell into receivership, lending credence to the rumor that the receivers would reopen the railroad to the mountain terminus.

In early May, railroad vice president J. B. Crooker announced that the line would be temporarily rebuilt to the second crossing of the Stillaguamish, 1¹/₂ miles above Robe, to retrieve five cars filled with shingles at that camp as well as some other material. The work was expected to take three or four weeks, and when the cars were removed, the temporary tracks would be recovered for use on additional sidetracks at the smelter and for spur lines to logging camps below the canyon.

Surveyors were still planning a new route around the flood-ravaged canyon. The new route would bring the tracks around to the right of the hill at Granite Falls and cut though the heavy timber well above the river to a point about 4 miles west of Silverton, where it would unite with the original tracks and cross bridge #30. This meant that the new tracks would join with the original tracks near Schweitzer Creek just east of the shoofly curve.

Not wanting to deal with delays in ore shipments, the 45 Mining Company solicited bids to haul 3,000 tons of stockpiled ore from the mine to the railroad at Sultan. An enterprising Silverton resident named Dan Sutherland saw a golden opportunity and opened the "Silverton, Mud Tunnel, and Great Western Railway" between Silverton and Bogardus,

Looking down the back side of Monte Cristo. Dumas Street ran along the front of these buildings, out of sight to the left. Perhaps the most interesting feature of this photo is the two-story outhouses, complete with catwalks from their attached buildings. The catwalks were probably built to accommodate the needs of residents during the long winter months, when snow could pile to depths of 15 feet. *(Enid Nordlund Collection)*

1 mile west of Gold Basin. At Bogardus, supplies and people were loaded onto an aerial tramway that crossed the river to the old tote wagon road on the west side. The officers and principals of the company were: President, Dan Sutherland; Conductor, Dan Sutherland; Brakeman, Dan Sutherland. On the way down, the *Everett Herald* said, "Isaac Newton fires up," but on the return to Silverton, "L. Bowgrease furnished the motive power.... The management guarantees more scenery, short curves, and hair breadth escapes to the rod than any other railroad in the United States." Yes, the locomotive was a handcar.

On July 1, 1898, the Everett and Monte Cristo Railway announced that it had won the bid to transport the 3,000 tons of stockpiled ore from the 45 Mine bunkers to the smelter in Everett, which meant that the railroad would have to be rebuilt at least temporarily to Silverton. But apparently the contract was never signed and the mining company removed the ore from the bunkers below Silverton and had it hauled out through the Sultan Basin to the Great Northern line.

On July 11, a fire that was ignited by a spark from a passing train destroyed the depot at Lowell. By mid-September, parties eager for the rebuilding of the line into the mountains were excited to learn that not only had the railroad followed up on the survey south of the river, but it was also conducting another one from Robe over Green Mountain and up Canyon Creek. As for the canyon, one engineer reportedly suggested that it was still a good place to run the railroad if the cribbing were securely attached to the rock walls and the roadbed was raised 5 or 6 feet. This, of course, would mean raising the ceiling of the tunnels 5 or 6 feet, which would be expensive.

The Rockefeller Power Play

The deeds for the major mines at Monte Cristo were turned over to the receivers on January 7, 1899. The Rockefeller syndicate held a majority ownership of the mines and railroad, but not quite everything. The Monte Cristo mines had never paid off for the owners for an assortment of reasons, and with the mines now dormant, Rockefeller had to cut his losses. It was in his best interest to rebuild the railroad, reopen the mines, and then sell. To reap the greatest profit from the sale, he had to squeeze out the remaining investors in the mines before rebuilding. One of Rockefeller's companies, which had advanced the Monte Cristo companies money during better times, pushed the mining companies into receivership. When the receiver's sale was held, the Rockefeller people bought the whole lot. In this way, they took a nearly worthless mining property and a badly damaged railroad and put themselves in a good position to turn a profit.

This maneuvering was not made public, of course, but many interested parties suspected it. When the news spread that the mines were securely in the hands of Rockefeller, many believed that the railroad would certainly be rebuilt and that the mines would reopen at once.

By mid-June 1899, trains were running between Everett and Robe, and tracklayers and construction crews were pushing past the mill toward Monte Cristo. That month, Rockefeller himself journeyed from New York to Everett in his own private Pullman car. He was expected to meet with James J. Hill, president of the Great Northern, to discuss Hill's purchase of the entire Rockefeller interest in the Everett and Monte Cristo area, including the railroad. The meeting bore no fruit, and no property changed hands. This left the Rockefeller syndicate in possession of the Mystery 1, 2, and 3 mines, along with the Pride of the Woods and the Pride of the Mountains. The Wilmans brothers retained ownership of the Golden Cord and Comet mines. Other owners clung to some of the smaller properties, such as the O&B.

4

The Northern Pacific Takes Over

In January 1900, Master Mechanic H. H. Warner of the Northern Pacific arrived in Everett to examine the defunct nailworks. Although the nailworks and the Everett and Monte Cristo were not directly related, the fact that Northern Pacific people were in the area excited many of the local residents, who hoped that the Northern Pacific would buy the Everett and Monte Cristo line. While the railroad appeared to be doing well, it was not. It was on the verge of bankruptcy.

On February 3, the Northern Pacific acquired the Everett and Monte Cristo's trackage from Everett to Snohomish—the old 3S portion of the line. The Northern Pacific president, Charles S. Mellen, said that the primary reason for the purchase was to secure more terminals for its growing Pacific coast business. Mellen had sent agents to appraise the line in 1899. James J. Hill, president of the Great Northern, warned Mellen that the line was not a worthy purchase, and he warned of potential legal wrangling over the 3S line formerly owned by the Everett and Monte Cristo in areas now contested by the Northern Pacific

The Everett Smelter viewed from the slough below it. On the two left-hand stacks are white "beards" deposited on the downwind side. These might have consisted of arsenic trioxide, a by-product of the roasting process that drove off the contaminants of arsenic and sulfur prior to smelting. Most of the ore from the Monte Cristo mines was smelted here, with the gold and silver drawn off as doré, a mixture of gold and silver. *(John A. Juleen photo)*

The slag heap at the base of the Everett Smelter. Still hot from the furnaces, it steamed as it cooled. In the mid-20th century, some of this slag was used to pave Everett's alleys. It was later found to contain large amounts of arsenic. The smelter site was converted to a residential neighborhood in the 1930s. Today it is a Superfund cleanup site because of the high levels of arsenic and other toxic compounds. *(Phil Woodhouse Collection)*

and the Great Northern. Mellen and Hill seldom saw eye to eye, and when Mellen ignored Hill's warnings, Hill appealed directly to J. P. Morgan, a heavy financial backer of the Northern Pacific, but to no avail.

Perhaps Mellen felt that it was an astute purchase, or perhaps he simply wanted to prove Hill wrong. In any event, ownership of the trackage changed from the Rockefeller interests to those of the Northern Pacific–controlled Seattle & International Railway (formerly the Seattle Lake Shore and Eastern). The price was $750,000. Mellen didn't inform Northern Pacific officials until September 1902. When he did, they were stunned by the news. Why Mellen was so secretive about the deal is not known. The sale was not finalized and publicly revealed in all its details until September 1903, when the line became the Monte Cristo branch of the Northern Pacific. No changes in operation were made immediately, but by the first week of October 1902, the Northern Pacific had closed the Monte Cristo depot at Snohomish and transferred all business there to its old Northern Pacific depot.

The Smelter Trust

The Guggenheims had made their money in the shirtwaist industry in New York City. They manufactured clothing from fine linen that they imported from their native Switzerland. The elder Guggenheim was not one to lend money, but if he saw a good business deal in the making, he would join as a partner. When a friend asked for a loan of $10,000 to rehabilitate a spent silver mine in Colorado, Guggenheim refused, but he did enter into a partnership in the venture. Inspectors had determined that if the mine were drained of water, it would produce again. The venture proved successful, but the local smelter charged a steep refining fee. Guggenheim quickly realized that money was to be made not in the mining but in the smelting and refining of the ore, so he bought the smelter.

Guggenheim eventually sold his clothing business in New York and bought smelters all over the world through his Smelter Trust, which later became the American Smelting and Refining Company (ASARCO). When the Smelter Trust sought to buy the smelter in Everett, John D. Rockefeller forced it to purchase the Monte Cristo mines as well. The Guggenheims quickly closed the mines and eventually divested themselves of them. They also purchased the Ruston Smelter in Tacoma. Not needing two smelters close together, they shut down the Everett smelter in 1910 and moved much of the machinery to Tacoma, most notably the arsenic roasting ovens and bag houses.

The newer bridge that carried the railway over the South Fork of the Stillaguamish River on its second crossing. The original bridge was a double-span Howe truss bridge that washed away in the 1897 flood. The added height of this bridge is apparent from the lower height of the original trestle approaches. *(Phil Woodhouse Collection)*

Service between Everett and Granite Falls continued in 1900, and one additional train was added between Everett and Snohomish. Trackage rights between Everett and Snohomish on the old 3S line had been retained by the Everett and Monte Cristo when it sold the former 3S line to the Northern Pacific, along with all rolling stock.

The sale built a fire under the rumor that a European syndicate that was planning to buy the smelter would soon purchase and open the line all the way to Monte Cristo. (The Guggenheim syndicate purchased the smelter in September 1903.) People also speculated that the new owners would reroute the railroad through Lake Stevens to Everett, thus shortening the line somewhat. (Although the more direct route between Everett and Lake Stevens was often mentioned, the way proved too steep to be practical.)

Also in February, the 45 Mining Company signed an agreement with the Puget Sound Reduction Company in which the latter would rebuild the railroad in exchange for the mining company's promise to ship a minimum of 3,000 tons of ore per month to the smelter. The repair work was to be completed on or before June 15, 1900.

On April 13, 1900, J. B. Crooker announced that the railroad would be rebuilt all the way to Monte Cristo. The work would be completed by June 1, and immediately thereafter Rockefeller would put the mines back into operation, employing 500 men and adding much-needed business to the railroad. As an added precaution against storms, the rails through tunnel #6 and other trouble spots would be embedded in concrete on a solid rock foundation. In places, the roadbed would be raised and wing dams installed to divert rushing floodwaters. The plans called for bridge #18 at the second crossing of the Stillaguamish River above Robe to be raised a little higher, and the two Howe truss throughspans would be replaced with one long span. The riverbed at that point would also be redirected to force water straight under the bridge instead of making a bend.

The Monte Cristo line just below the town of Robe in Robe Canyon. The rails were set in concrete to prevent them from washing away during the floods that often caused the Stillaguamish River to flow through tunnel #6 (shown in the distance). This photo looks down the tracks toward Granite Falls. *(Enid Nordlund Collection, John A. Juleen photo)*

By May 1900, the snow was melting fast in the mountains, and mining and prospecting activities were about a month ahead of usual, generating optimism in the mountain hamlets. On May 19, the entire population of Silverton turned out for a gala celebration at the railroad depot as the first train in nearly three years approached. Blasts of Giant (brand) powder filled the mountain air. (Giant powder was a somewhat unstable but very effective mixture of nitroglycerine and black powder used in the mines.) Speeches were made, poems recited, and Superintendent Foster gave three cheers for Queen Victoria. Engineer Sutton wore his best clothes, and Dan Sutherland fell into the river.

Soon Monte Cristo was again the end of the line for the railroad. On August 25, the company was reorganized with new officers and "Everett" was dropped from the name, reflecting the fact that the Everett to Snohomish trackage had been sold to the Northern Pacific. The railroad was renamed the Monte Cristo Railway Company.

New Management

The first big news for the railroad in 1901 was the resignation of J. B. Crooker (known as Papa Crooker) as general manager. Crooker was a religious man who had steadfastly refused to allow excursions to Monte Cristo on Sundays. A few months later, J. O. Whitmarsh was appointed the new general superintendent of the railroad. More summer activities were planned, including Sunday school outings for Snohomish area residents.

On July 14, 1901, regular excursion trains began running, leaving Riverside Station (Pacific Avenue Station) at 8 a.m. and arriving at Monte Cristo about 11:00 a.m. There the passengers would disembark and walk to a 50-by-100-foot platform at Sunday Flats complete with seats and tables and a magnificent view of Sunday Falls. (Sunday Flats was the upper-class part of town, where most of the mining company officials and superintendents lived.) The return trip left at 4 p.m. and arrived in Everett at 7 p.m.

What made the excursions especially popular were the open observation cars that offered unobstructed views as the train made its way through the dense forest, open farm country, and the deep and picturesque canyon beyond Granite Falls and along the Stillaguamish River. These observation cars, a rarity for any railroad, were little more than flat cars with seats attached.

Two incidents served to temper the euphoria, however. On the western edge of the Monte Cristo line on the night of September 2, the business district of Hartford went up in flames. Lost were Barney Lee's Hotel and Saloon, Phillips' General Merchandise store, the post office, and several other stores and residences. A few days later, the lumber kiln at Robe was lost to a fire that destroyed 60,000 feet of lumber. Such fires were common in those times because of the lack of firefighting equipment and the remoteness of the sites.

At the end of September 1901, snow descended on Monte Cristo and Superintendent Whitmarsh announced plans to retain daily service along the route all winter if possible. Passenger coaches would be combined with freight trains, and the big rotary plow would travel in the morning ahead of the first train and return that evening to meet the afternoon train. The plow had to be used with care because when it hit rocks or trees in the snowdrifts, the blades were often damaged. The blades entered the drifts at a rate of 300 rpm, and sudden impact with a rock or tree could cause the knives to rip loose from the rotor and sail through the air.

Whitmarsh also reported that the roadbed, with its new riprapping, was ready for the

floods. But floods seemed unlikely that year. The October snowfall was most feared, because November would bring the warm winds from the southwest, melting the snow and causing flooding. But this year, most of the snow had already melted and no new snow fell in October.

Things were going well along the railroad. The Independent Mine at Silverton was planning to build a large concentrating mill at the edge of town. Residences and hotels in the camp were full, and new ones were being built. Surveyors for the Bonanza Queen Mine on Deer Creek planned to work all winter. The 45 Mine was shipping ore regularly and planned to continue all winter.

By Christmas, a shed that was supposed to withstand the 18 to 20 feet of snow that usually fell each winter protected the turntable at Monte Cristo.

A New Beginning

Business was brisk along the Monte Cristo line all the way from Hartford Junction to Monte Cristo in early 1902. Lumber mills were in full swing, the mines were developing their properties, and unemployment was near zero. At Silverton, residents were excited that the Copper Independent Mine was planning to put its large concentrator on the flats just west of town.

On May 19, daily round-trip freight and passenger service began between Everett and Monte Cristo. Passengers and mail from Seattle could make the connection with the Monte

Just outside the eastern portal of tunnel #6, workmen prepare forms for encasing the timber cribbing in concrete. Floods in Robe Canyon frequently destroyed the cribbing. The solution was to encase the whole line in concrete. This technique worked for the remainder of the line's operating life. In the winter of 1996, landslides finally broke some of the concrete loose from the right-of-way. *(Everett Public Library Collection; photographer unknown, but possibly Herman Siewart)*

Cristo excursion train in Everett and enjoy the scenery in one long day of travel. On July 1, a postal car complete with a post office clerk was included for mail distribution along the route. Previously, only mail pouches had been used, delaying return mail between railroad stops by a day.

On May 21, 1902, a train described as "practically new throughout" left the station in Everett for the mountain terminus. The cars had been repaired and completely refurbished. The #99 locomotive (formerly #4) that pulled it was the first to bear the new company logo, painted in a gilt color against the dark brown of the locomotive and tender. The logo was a double circle enclosing an interlocking MC monogram, which was surrounded by the legend "Scenic Line of the Northwest." Locomotive #99 was an American type 4-4-0 (See photo on page 52.).

The first Sunday excursion of the year left on June 8 from Riverside Station in Everett. Two well-equipped observation cars and six regular coaches were added to the train. At Monte Cristo, the pavilion at Sunday Flats was put in shape for the coming tourist excursions. The excursion on Sunday, July 13, was billed as the largest that season. Nine coaches and two observation cars afforded ample accommodations for the 500 passengers as well as a brass band.

Excursions of this time often included unscheduled stops along the way to allow fishermen and sightseers to disembark, picking them up on the return trip. Sometimes the trains would even wait while a photographer set up camera equipment for a shot of the train.

Locomotive #366, a Ten Wheeler, arrives at Hartford Junction in 1910. The Northern Pacific operated the line as the Monte Cristo branch during this time. This locomotive is the reshopped #1 of the Everett and Monte Cristo Railway, which was built by the Cooke Locomotive Works of Paterson, New Jersey. It appears that all of the depot personnel emerged to pose for this photo. *(Enid Nordlund Collection)*

Granite Falls in 1910, looking westward. Locomotive #366, the Northern Pacific's redesignation of the Everett and Monte Cristo's #1, is headed toward Robe Canyon and Monte Cristo. This Ten Wheeler (4-6-0) was reshopped and given a new electrical system. The acetylene headlamp was replaced by a smaller, more powerful electric headlamp atop the smoke box. The locomotive also sported running lamps. Notice the horse-drawn carriage parked near the large milk cans that were used to ship milk up and down the line. *(Enid Nordlund Collection)*

Mining Ends at Monte Cristo

Rain in December 1902 caused an unusual New Year's for the passengers on the Monte Cristo Branch of the Northern Pacific. On December 31, the train from Monte Cristo encountered a huge mud and rockslide between tunnels #2 and #3 as it descended through Robe Canyon toward Granite Falls. With the tracks completely blocked for 200 feet, the crew and passengers were forced to spend the night and most of New Year's Day aboard the train while a crew cleared the tracks.

(following page) Tunnel #5, the shortest on the line, pierces a headland above the Stillaguamish River in Robe Canyon. This photo was taken either during or after the Northern Pacific's ownership, because during this period the concrete retaining walls were placed over the log cribbing. Notice the tracks on the other side of the tunnel as well as on the near side. *(Enid Nordlund Collection)*

The floods that followed were considered the worst since 1896-97, with the tracks between Lowell and Snohomish again under water. Anyone traveling from Everett to any point beyond Hartford had to go by boat to Snohomish, by train to Hartford, and then walk the rest of the way. Damage along the Monte Cristo line prevented trains from traveling beyond Hartford. But due to the extensive work done in the canyon by the company in 1900, nowhere near the damage of 1896-1897 was done. Repairs were made quickly, and trains soon ran all the way to Monte Cristo. While rain had been the problem in the lowlands, snow in the mountains was causing difficulty.

The train to Monte Cristo on February 11, 1903, became snowbound at Silverton and two days later was reported to be somewhere between Barlow Pass and Monte Cristo. The big rotary plow had been moved to the Pacific Division of the Northern Pacific, leaving the Monte Cristo train at the mercy of the elements. After a delay of more than three days, the train finally arrived back in Everett after ramming through the snow on its own.

A near-fatal accident occurred on the last day of February when a freight train coming down from Monte Cristo was struck by a large boulder that dropped onto the tracks near the mouth of tunnel #3. The rock rolled under the pilot, damaging the lower structure of the locomotive before the train could stop. This was quickly followed by a slide that hit two cars behind the tender and pushed them over to the side, where they hung out over the wall above the raging river. Two days later the cars and locomotive were rerailed and operation continued.

More problems arose when the March 10 train failed to reach Monte Cristo because of heavy snow. The rotary plow that preceded the train broke down at Silverton. With repairs to the plow expected to take a

Tunnel #5 on the Northern Pacific's Monte Cristo branch glows in the light of a late summer's day. The concrete retaining walls, installed by the Northern Pacific, protected the log cribbing beneath. *(Phil Woodhouse Collection)*

The turntable at Monte Cristo was turned using what was jokingly called the "armstrong method." A 68½-ton locomotive was rolled onto the table and rotated by hand. A latching device ensured that the table stopped at the correct position and that it did not move once positioned. By 1927, when this photo was taken, steam locomotives no longer serviced the area, so only gas cars needed to be turned around. *(Dorothy VanNorman photo)*

few days and the road blocked ahead by deep drifts, the train was forced to return to Everett. The plow had reluctantly been brought back from the Northern Pacific's Pacific Division to service the Monte Cristo line after residents up the line complained to the railroad company.

Soon the tracks were cleared all the way to the end of the line, and service was restored to Monte Cristo. But on April 15, the train failed to return to Everett from the mountain terminus. It had reached Monte Cristo without incident, but on the way back it encountered a snowslide across the tracks between Barlow Pass and Silverton. Unfortunately, the rotary plow was back in the Cascade Division that night. A portion of the next morning was spent clearing the rails, and the train reached Everett early the next day.

As the snow receded in the spring warmth, the Northern Pacific was determined to improve the condition of the Monte Cristo branch. To this end, it let a contract to the Pacific Coast Construction Company of Oregon to make extensive improvements. A crew of 25 filled in bridges, straightened curves, and replaced culverts with 24-inch sewer pipe.

When the Northern Pacific first bought the Monte Cristo line, rumors began circulating that this would ultimately become part of the transcontinental line because it would be the shortest route across the mountains and presented the easiest crossing. With the heavy work being done on the line, this theory was once again revived.

In September 1903, the Federal Mining & Smelting Company sold the Everett Smelter and Monte Cristo mines to ASARCO—a move that would ultimately have a devastating effect on the Monte Cristo branch of the Northern Pacific. For some time, ASARCO had wanted to buy the smelter, both for the equipment and to eliminate the competition with its Tacoma smelter. Although ASARCO had no interest in operating the mines, Rockefeller made the mines an inseparable part of the deal. If they wanted to buy the smelter, they had to buy the mines. Almost immediately, ASARCO permanently shut down the Monte Cristo mines. In Everett, the first sign that something was amiss came when laid-off miners began arriving from Monte Cristo. On November 30, the mines closed and the task of removing equipment from them began. The concentrator remained in operation for about two weeks to process the ore that was already on the dump, and then it, too, closed.

Quieter Times

As 1904 began, the Monte Cristo mines remained closed and the 45 Mine at Silverton was in receivership. But business was booming in Silverton with the shipment of the first carload of concentrates from the Independent Mining Company's new concentrator. The new mill not only processed ore for the company, as its counterpart at Monte Cristo did, but it also provided a rare commodity for such a remote mining camp: electricity. Some 300 residents of the town enjoyed this new luxury.

On January 14, 1904, a huge mudslide tore out 300 feet of track near the shoofly curve 6 miles west of Silverton, cutting off access east of there by train. The damage was soon repaired and trains again ran through to Monte Cristo. But by March 1, snow blocked the tracks again between Silverton and Monte Cristo, and service was cut off. With the Northern Pacific reluctant to move the rotary plow off its Cascade routes and return it to Monte Cristo, the little hamlet remained snowbound and isolated for about a month. On rare occasions, residents made the grueling hike out to Silverton for mail. But that was the extent of communications with the outside world.

A rotary plow was made available on April 1 for the Monte Cristo route, and the tracks were plowed all the way through, followed by a passenger train. At Monte Cristo, the crew discovered $5^1/_2$ feet of snow. The roof over the turntable had collapsed under the weight of the heavy accumulation. It was never rebuilt. The snow and debris were laboriously cleared to put the turntable back in operation. The 20 or 30 remaining inhabitants welcomed the end of their isolation. The winter schedule was then put back into effect, with trains running to Monte Cristo three times a week.

Nichols' Store at Stead, just up the tracks from the town of Robe. A typical country store, it stocked almost every necessity. *(Enid Nordlund Collection)*

The Granite Falls depot in the 1910s, when the Northern Pacific operated the line as the Monte Cristo branch. The milk containers lined up against the building are waiting to be picked up by local retailers or sent back down the line. The train is a combination consist, composed of freight cars followed by passenger coaches. *(Phil Woodhouse Collection)*

Sightseers at the entrance of tunnel #4. Behind them is tunnel #5, just a short distance up the tracks. Robe Canyon, with its rapids and tight turns of the rails, was a favorite with visitors. This group apparently decided to do it the hard way. They sit on what appears to be a handcar (or a speeder). When the railway was idle, all kinds of rolling stock were used to gain access to the mountains. *(Enid Nordlund Collection)*

As the snow began to melt, lowland residents as well as tourist businesses in the mountains waited for the ever-popular summer excursions to begin. But the Northern Pacific now owned the railroad lock, stock, and barrel, and the company was not about to invest in excursions. All extra passenger cars were pulled off lesser routes to handle increased traffic in the Midwest for the St. Louis Fair in Missouri. While Sunday excursions were not taboo, they were to be run only on special occasions or for important public events.

The old syndicate mines at Monte Cristo remained idle, although ASARCO did bring in mining experts from other areas to look over the properties, renewing hopes that the mines would soon reopen.

More Troubles

While disaster was no stranger to the Monte Cristo line, few had lost their lives there. But that changed on February 5, 1905, and continued over the next few weeks. As a work train backed up the canyon near tunnel #2 in the late afternoon, the tender left the tracks for some

The Northern Pacific's locomotive #366 pauses before entering the western portal of tunnel #3 in Robe Canyon. This locomotive, formerly the Everett and Monte Cristo Railway's locomotive #1, along with locomotives #367 (E&MC #2), #368 (E&MC #3), and #649 (E&MC #99), continued to serve the Northern Pacific. The winter weather seldom caused much trouble in the canyon, where elevations were below 600 feet. *(Enid Nordlund Collection)*

(previous page) Silverton in the halcyon years. Silver Gulch forms the backdrop. On the far right is the Copper Independent Mine's concentrator building; on the left is the steel truss bridge across the Stillaguamish River. In the foreground are the tracks of the Monte Cristo branch of the Northern Pacific, running to Monte Cristo to the left and Robe and Granite Falls to the right. *(Enid Nordlund Collection)*

Silverton in the 1920s sported a steel truss bridge across the Stillaguamish River. The railroad tracks ran up the left bank of the river. The lower slopes of Long Mountain form the backdrop. *(Granite Falls Historical Society Collection)*

unknown reason, crashing onto its side. This pulled the locomotive onto its side across the tracks, knocking the cab loose and wedging it between the tender and the boiler. Six men were trapped inside. The impact broke steam pipes, which scalded the trapped men. The caboose was also thrown across the tracks but was not upset, sparing injury to the conductor and others inside.

The men trapped in the locomotive included the fireman, who died within minutes. The engineer, who received a full blast of steam square in the face, suffered for more than 10 hours before succumbing to his injuries. It had been his first trip since being hospitalized for broken bones. Three bridgemen and the engine watchman were taken to Seattle, all in critical condition. Three days later, the watchman died, followed by one of the bridgemen on February 10. No explanation for the accident was ever found.

Spring brought more speculation that the Northern Pacific would extend the Monte Cristo line over the mountains because the railroad had put a large crew to work on the right-of-way. Although the railroad passed it off as no big deal, the tracks were fitted for heavier traffic and the roadbed was widened.

In the spring, the 45 Mining Company, which had been idle for a couple of years while in receivership, started pumping water out of its workings. At the Bonanza Queen Mine, a new power plant was nearly completed, and workers were back in the mine. Plans for a tramway from the mine to the railroad were also made.

July 6, 1905, brought another serious accident in the Stillaguamish Canyon, where a crew was replacing and double-shoring the timbering in trouble-plagued tunnel #4. The scaffolding they were standing on gave way, sending them plummeting to the tracks some 8 feet below. One man suffered temporary damage to his spine, and another was slightly injured; the rest of the crew was badly shaken. (Tunnel #4 and tunnel #2 had been the sites of numerous rockslides in the past and presented an almost constant challenge to repair crews.)

In mid-September, the railroad announced that by winter the road would be in good enough condition to guarantee uninterrupted service. Crews continued to work on the roadbed and began installing retaining walls to lessen damage from rockslides and mudslides. This boast was soon challenged when an early October storm dropped the heaviest rainfall on Monte Cristo since the big 1897 storm. But the right-of-way was not significantly damaged. However, telegraph and telephone service was knocked out between Monte Cristo, Silverton, and Robe.

New Business, New Struggles

Although the major mines at Monte Cristo had been shut down since November 1903, in November 1905 the Wilmans brothers confirmed that they had taken possession of the dormant mines. They said that they would reopen those workings along with the Rainy and Monte Cristo claims and would rebuild the concentrator and add a cyanide plant. (The Monte Cristo claims, which included the famous Comet Mine, were among the earliest mining properties in the camp and had been owned by the Wilmans brothers from the outset. These were separate from the big syndicate mines—the Mystery and Pride groups—which were often referred to as the Monte Cristo Claims.) This, along with a recent large ore discovery in their Justice Mine, could guarantee needed business for the railroad.

The Bonanza Queen Mine near Silverton reported that beginning in May, it would ship at least one carload of ore per day to the smelter. Along with the new summer railroad

Workers double-shore tunnel #4 on the Monte Cristo branch of the Northern Pacific. The fragile rock caused continuous problems in the early years. This was one attempt to stem the hillside's movement. *(Enid Nordlund Collection)*

schedule for the Northern Pacific branch lines, the company considered offering special rates for fishermen, who would be dropped off at their favorite fishing holes on the way up and picked up on the return trip that evening.

The hot, dry summer provided a little extra excitement for Silverton residents when, in early August, 1906, a forest fire broke out 2^1/$_2$ miles below town because of a spark from a passing locomotive. The fire wiped out a good stand of timber and threatened to sweep through the town. Fortunately, the wind changed direction and the flames shifted in the opposite direction, but not before it had sent 10 or 12 trees crashing across the tracks. Some were as large as 6 feet in diameter and had to be dynamited off the rails.

When the timbers at the western end of tunnel #1 burned in 1907, the unconsolidated rock and loose soil collapsed into the bore. About 400 feet of the 833-foot tunnel was dug through unstable material. This photo shows piping and monitor nozzles, which were usually used in placer mining. A steam pump used for firefighting at the Rucker brothers' Lake Stevens Mill was hauled up the line and powered by steam from one of the locomotives. This photo was taken from the deck of the 150-foot Howe truss bridge across the Stillaguamish River and looks straight at the collapsed portal. Water was being pumped through the pipes at the left and right of the photo and was directed toward the soft, caved material via the monitors. A large amount of the debris was thus washed away in a short time, allowing a timely reconstruction of the tunnel and reopening of the line into Robe Canyon. *(Enid Nordlund Collection)*

Later that month, a passenger train bound for Monte Cristo slammed head-on into a westbound freight train at Lowell. Luckily, both trains were traveling slowly, and the damage was not enough to put them out of commission. Most of the passengers continued on to their destinations, with only three of them suffering bumps and bruises.

October brought more inclement weather to the region, and passengers coming into Everett on the Monte Cristo train reported that the Stillaguamish Canyon was full for miles, with the water only a foot or two below the tracks in places. On December 28, a large slide covered the tracks near tunnel #2. Rocks and dirt slid unhindered from above, and as quickly as the crews worked, the tracks were again buried. The right-of-way was

Tunnel #1 was about 833 feet long. The last half was bored through solid rock and presented few maintenance problems. The first half, however, was tunneled through soft earth and loose boulders. Periodically, sparks from the coal-burning locomotives ignited the supporting timbers and the roof would come crashing down, blocking the line a few miles above the town of Granite Falls. For this photo, the photographer stood on the 150-foot deck span Howe truss bridge on which the line made its first crossing of the Stillaguamish River. The photo looks up the line toward where the portal of tunnel #1 once stood. Fire had consumed the timbers and closed the line. The section crews are shown removing debris. Notice the barrels on platforms on the side of the bridge (to the right of center). These held water to fight fires on the bridge or in the tunnel. They were useful only if a crew member spotted the fire and stopped the train. Often the train was long gone by the time the fire got underway. *(Enid Nordlund Collection)*

The mill town of Robe, just above Robe Canyon, sometime between 1900 and 1905. Founded by Truitt K. Robe as the location of his Canyon Lumber Company, the town relied on the railroad to get supplies in and its products out. As time passed, however, the market demand for long timbers grew. Because of the tight turns and tunnels in Robe Canyon, the railroad refused to carry anything that could not fit into a boxcar. This forced the Canyon Lumber Company to move to Everett, and the town of Robe gradually died. *(Enid Nordlund Collection)*

Straining every side rod, this locomotive tackles the final grade to Barlow Pass. This combination freight and passenger train was typical of the consists that traveled the line around the turn of the century. *(Enid Nordlund Collection)*

covered for 200 feet, with debris 20 feet deep. A special train had to be dispatched to tunnel #2 to transfer passengers and express over the slide from the train stuck above the slide.

The slide menaced workmen until January 8, 1907, when the tracks were finally cleared and trains again traveled the entire length of the railway. During the two-week period that the tracks were blocked, trains on the east and west sides of the slide transferred passengers and cargo between each other across the impasse by foot.

In early 1907, sparks from a passing locomotive set timbers in tunnel #1 on fire at both ends of the bore. The heavy wood shoring was destroyed and the earth and rock began to tumble in, caving the entire tunnel almost from end to end. A locomotive and snowplow were trapped on the upstream side. Ticket sales were suspended for points above the tunnel while repairs were made. In the meantime, mills, mines, and logging camps above tunnel #1 became idle. Trains carried the mail once a week to the tunnel, where the sacks were hand-carried up the almost sheer cliff and over the top of the hill to the other side, where the trapped train would take it along the line above the collapsed tunnel.

Soon the mail service above tunnel #1 was also suspended because the locomotive trapped upstream from the bore was nearly out of coal. The last trip to Monte Cristo was on February 2. With this disheartening news, residents of the upstream communities rushed to get needed supplies on this last train.

In the meantime, the Northern Pacific reported that hydraulic sluicing equipment had been moved to the tunnel to remove the large quantities of mud and sand. May 27 was a jubilant day for the isolated residents above tunnel #1. The first train in nearly four months chugged up the valley to the settlements. Tunnel #1 was said to be as good as new.

On May 31, 1907, the first carload of ore from the Monte Cristo mines since the fall of 1903 arrived by train at the Everett smelter. As more mines along the route got into full operation that summer, the shipments increased. By September, three trains a week ran to Monte Cristo. The concentrator there had been remodeled, with a new section added and an enormous amount of new machinery inside. The mines, which had been sold by the Wilmans brothers to a Mr. Silverman in 1906, were in full swing, and the old shacks in the town were replaced with more substantial buildings. The company was building new homes for miners.

Elsewhere along the line, the old mill town of Robe was aspiring to become a tourist resort. Construction began on a large, well-appointed hotel, to the tune of $7,000. The Arlington Lumber Company announced that it would build a combination saw and shingle mill in Gold Basin, a small mining hamlet above the sec-

Barlow Pass in about 1918. A Hartford Eastern gas car heads toward Monte Cristo on a fine summer day. The building next to the car is the Penn Mining Company's warehouse. The building behind the car is the new U.S. Forest Service guard station. At Barlow Pass, the line crossed from the watershed of the Stillaguamish River to that of the Sauk River. Sheep Mountain graces the skyline. *(John A. Juleen photo)*

ond crossing of the Stillaguamish River. The combined daily capacity of the mills would be 30,000 feet of lumber and 120,000 shingles.

On November 21, 1907, as if to mock the railroad's earlier efforts, another slide about 30 feet long and 4 feet deep covered the tracks near tunnel #1, delaying traffic for some time. On February 17, 1908, yet another rockslide covered the tracks, this time about a mile east of tunnel #1. For a while, no passengers, express, or perishable freight could travel above Wayside, a small mining camp west of the first crossing of the

The Penn Mining Company's warehouse at Barlow Pass in very deep snow. *(U.S. Forest Service, Darrington Ranger District)*

Tunnel #4 appears high above the level of the Stillaguamish River in Robe Canyon. While this tunnel did not suffer attack by the river, the weak rock through which it was bored often crumbled. Several section hands were killed or injured while clearing landslide and collapse debris. When double-shoring the bore did not solve the problem, the Northern Pacific blew the roof off the bore in the summer of 1911. *(Walt Meglasson Collection)*

Stillaguamish River. To add to the problem, snow blocked the tracks just below Silverton. By the end of February 1908, service was restored to Robe. After more snow blockages in March and April, on April 18 the first train of the year chugged into Monte Cristo. There the crew found 3 to 4 feet of snow and only two or three families who had remained in the camp over the winter.

Because railroad service was about to be limited to Silverton, on October 31, 1908, the final Monte Cristo train carried a large amount of freight for wintering residents. At Barlow Pass, a large landslide delayed the train for several hours, and it did not arrive back in Everett until 3 a.m. on Sunday. With Silverton now the railroad terminus for the winter, a postman on snowshoes transported mail from there to Monte Cristo twice a week. He hiked from Monte Cristo on Mondays and Fridays and left Silverton on Tuesdays and Saturdays.

In January 1909, another mammoth rockslide buried the tracks in Robe Canyon. This time it was at tunnel #4, and it blocked traffic on the line for a month. It was about 200 feet long and 25 feet deep and was the result of a massive Chinook wind with heavy rain that caused extensive flooding in the lowlands. As 20 or so men removed the debris from the tracks, other, smaller slides came down on them, which made for frustrating and hazardous work. In mid-February, they finished their work and trains began traveling unimpeded between Everett and Robe.

By mid-May of 1909, the right-of-way was free of snow all the way to Monte Cristo except for a drift at Barlow Pass. However promising this news was, Northern Pacific soon threw a wrench into the plans of tourists who wanted to take the summer excursion trains; it announced in early June that trains would probably not run past Silverton unless the mines at Monte Cristo were back in operation. The railroad said that Everettites gave the line too little patronage and that the roadbed was in too poor condition to permit travel. A railroad worker who passed over the route on a speeder challenged the railroad's contention, but the summer schedule was cut back anyway. The train traveled to Granite Falls every day, to Robe three times a week, and all the way to Silverton on Saturdays.

In late spring, a group of Snohomish men purchased from the Forest Service all the merchantable timber along the Monte Cristo line near the headwaters of the Stillaguamish River below Barlow Pass. The group had been planning to erect a large mill plant at Gold Basin between Bogardus and Silverton.

On October 1, 1909, the first train in almost a year reached Monte Cristo unannounced. It carried railroad officials, and no reason for the tour was given. They might have been considering reopening the road in the event of a reestablishment of mining. In early November, the Imperial Mining Company of Silverton arranged for a special train so that prospective investors could inspect its holdings, which included more than 2,000 feet of tunneling, huge timber stands, a 300-ton-per-day concentrating mill, and a 1 1/2 mile water flume recently purchased from the old Independent Mining Company to conduct water to the mill. The investors had been lured there by advertisements that extolled the grand prospects of the property. The train remained in town for three hours while the mine's features were touted by mining company officials. Little investment was ever realized from this excursion.

Later that month, the seemingly seasonal Chinook winds and rain caused a series of washouts on the line once again. Most of the damage, as usual, was in Robe Canyon.

Toward a More Substantial Line

In January 1910, a work train and crew began working eastward from Granite Falls, repairing the damaged line as far as

This photo, which looks through tunnel #4 at tunnel #5, tells quite a story. The rock through which tunnel #4 was bored proved to be unstable and badly fractured. The shoring in the tunnel often shifted, sending tons of rock crashing onto the tracks. Several section hands lost their lives clearing landslides at this spot. Horizontal braces were placed across the tunnel at the top of the vertical timbering. This prevented large locomotives and tall rolling stock from passing. During this period, possibly around 1909-10, only light traffic used this part of the line. In the summer of 1911, the Northern Pacific closed the line and blasted the top off of this tunnel and tunnel #2, converting them into open cuts. *(Wallace and Callaway photo)*

Looking across the millpond at the lumber mill at Gold Basin (between Verlot and Red Bridge). This was one of the many mills along the line that relied on the railroad to transport products to market. *(U.S. Forest Service, Darrington Ranger District)*

Silverton. At tunnel #2 in the canyon, another crew prepared to eliminate the troublesome bore by removing the top and making it into an open cut. By mid-April, crews were still working on the line because the railroad believed that the Monte Cristo mines would reopen and the dormant mining camp would return to life. Passenger and freight trains ran as far as Gold Basin, and work trains carried heavy timbers beyond to the troublesome sinkhole 3 miles below Silverton, where a pile bridge would replace the "moving scenery" that carried away several rods of track the previous winter. (A rod, which equals $16\frac{1}{2}$ feet or $5\frac{1}{2}$ yards, was a common unit of measure at the time.) The roadmaster was under orders to push repairs as fast as weather would allow. Snow remained on the ground in places, with $4\frac{1}{2}$ feet at Barlow Pass and a record amount for that time of year at Monte Cristo. Near Robe, crews shored up bridge #16 by installing new stringers and ties.

The Gold Basin millpond as seen from the mill. Logs were soaked in the artificial pond to clean off dirt and rocks, which could quickly dull the big saw blades. The soaking also loosened the bark for easier removal by high-pressure water sprays. *(U.S. Forest Service, Darrington Ranger District)*

In late May, another enormous slide of rock and sand came thundering down the hillside at tunnel #4 in the canyon, completely blocking the bore. Some of the boulders were said to be half the size of a boxcar. In spite of these setbacks, by June 7 the right-of-way had been cleared, and trains once again operated as far as Gold Basin. But in the first week of October, another big slide closed tunnel #4, causing the upper Stillaguamish communities to be cut off from rail service for several days.

No sooner had tunnel #4 been cleared than another calamity struck the line. At tunnel #2, a slide punctured and filled the bore with rocks and dirt, again blocking the right-of-way. This stoppage happened at a bad time of the year for the merchants, mills, and residents above the canyon because they were in the process of hauling in their winter supplies.

Although it was rumored all summer that an option had been taken by a big New York party to buy the Monte Cristo mines with the intent of reopening them, nothing came of it. The Northern Pacific halted all repair work on its tracks above Robe, stating that not enough commerce existed above that point to justify further expense.

As 1911 began, the railroad remained closed above Granite Falls until a final decision could be made on a remedy for the semiannual washouts and slides. Commerce upstream ground almost to a halt. Residents who depended on the line expected the Northern Pacific to keep it in operation. Railroad officials knew that they had to cut repair costs by thoroughly revamping the road. The plans for the summer included clearing the badly caved tunnel #2 and completing removing its top to make the tunnel into a large, deep open cut that would be easier to maintain.

Locals hoped that the line would be cleared all the way to Silverton by August. But no plans were announced to clear the tracks all the way into Monte Cristo. As August came and went, the line remained closed, even to Robe, while 100 workmen blasted and labored along the tracks, clearing slides, removing debris, and reballasting the roadbed. In mid-October, the line was finally open as far as Robe. Tunnels #2 and #4 had been blasted away and reduced to open cuts. Two weeks later, Gold Basin became the end of the line, with a train running there every Wednesday. Beyond Silverton, the tracks were reportedly clear of rocks and debris

A landslide in Robe Canyon blocks the Monte Cristo line. The Stillaguamish River carved this canyon through the unstable bedrock between the towns of Granite Falls and Robe. The railroad was built along one side of this canyon. Landslides of broken rock and soil were commonplace, especially during rainy or freezing weather. The slides were cleared with pick, shovel, and wheelbarrow.

all the way to Monte Cristo, and a handcar had run on that stretch of rail several times over the summer. Still, Monte Cristo remained nearly deserted, with only a few hardy souls doing assessment work on their claims.

November 1911 brought high water and resulting slides along the line. After only one train reached the town of Silverton, rock and debris slides covered the tracks in several locations in the canyon, especially in the area of the tunnel #2 open cut. The area above the canyon was once again cut off from rail service.

Tunnel #2 after its conversion to an open cut. This photo was taken in the 1920s, when the Hartford Eastern served the Inn at Big Four. This scene looks down the tracks toward the town of Granite Falls. *(John A. Juleen photo)*

By the third week of January 1912, the line was again open as far as Silverton, which enjoyed train service every Wednesday. The next month, word spread that a gasoline motor service would carry excursion parties from the waterfront to Monte Cristo. The service had already been tried on the Northern Pacific's tracks between Arlington and Darrington. The roadbed from Silverton to Monte Cristo was not in bad condition, considering that it hadn't been used for several years, and according to railroad officials, the only real problems over the past two years had been in the area of the Sinkhole.

On November 30, 1912, the railroad made the big announcement that the line would indeed be rebuilt all the way to Monte Cristo, and that in 1913 the hamlet would see its first train in several years. One hundred men were employed at tunnel #1 alone, while others relaid ties and placed them in concrete at several locations. General ballasting and repair work, mostly between Granite Falls and Gold Basin, was in progress. A 1,650-foot section of the tracks was laid in concrete from just outside of the west end of tunnel #6 to near Robe. This included the tracks in the tunnel itself, which were often flooded during severe storms. (The concrete trackbed remains in place today.)

This was great news for one of the mining companies near Monte Cristo. For three years, the Del Campo Mining Company, 3 miles west of town, had laboriously hauled supplies and equipment over the poorly maintained roadbed from Silverton to its camp using a railroad flat car pulled by mule power.

But the railroad company could only do so much. With much of the roadbed stabilized and new retaining walls and riprapping in place, everyone was confident that the line could remain open. They could not, however, control the unstable cliffs and avalanche tracks that were situated perilously above the railroad tracks.

The Northern Pacific Pulls Back

In December 1912, a big snowstorm cut off rail service above Robe. By January 1913, 7 feet of snow covered the ground at Silverton. A traveler reported that it took him two days to break a trail from Silverton to Robe and that the tracks in the canyon below Robe were blocked by slides in several places. Supplies began to run short for settlers living beyond Robe. As the situation worsened, calls for help were sent to the railroad. Apparently, no response came.

Finally, the frantic, isolated residents above Robe filed a complaint with the Washington State Public Service Commission. This government body ordered the Northern Pacific to immediately take steps to resume rail service as far as Silverton. The complaint to the commission stated that feed and groceries were nearly exhausted and that several families who wanted to leave on foot were prevented from doing so by the deep snow. It also stated that the railroad was making no effort to relieve the situation. The railroad president responded by lamenting

Tunnel #2 as an open cut, viewed from the approximate location of the old western portal. The suspension bridge from the limestone mining operation located across the Stillaguamish River can be seen through the cut. *(Walt Meglassen Collection)*

A charge of black powder is set off to pulverize the roof of tunnel #4 in Robe Canyon. In 1911, the Northern Pacific removed the roofs of tunnels #2 and #4, which were plagued by landslides and cave-ins. *(Enid Nordlund Collection)*

the expense, but the railroad sent a rotary plow to clear the line from Robe to Silverton.

Soon Snohomish County commissioners asked the Public Service Commission for help in inducing the Northern Pacific to resume rail traffic all the way to Monte Cristo. No scheduled trains had run beyond Silverton since 1908, when Sam Silverman's Monte Cristo Metals Company ceased operations and fell into receivership. The commissioners stated that several companies and individuals wanted to resume operations near Monte Cristo and that the county wanted to rebuild the bridge on the main street of Monte Cristo. They would need access via the railroad to do so.

To augment the commissioners' request, John F. Birney, former Snohomish County engineer, presented a nearly completed lease agreement to reopen the mines at Monte Cristo. Birney was interested in reopening some of the old Rockefeller mines there, especially the old Rainy Mine. His plan appeared to hinge on the successful reopening of the railroad to Monte Cristo. Because of the lease, the commissioners assured Birney that Northern Pacific would rebuild the railroad. The lease would show both the state and the railroad that the shippers needed the line for transportation. Birney said that he expected to ship ore to the Tacoma smelter within 60 days if the railroad was repaired to Monte Cristo. In

Tunnel #4 in 1911 after the roof was demolished by explosives. Workers dumped all of the debris into the Stillaguamish River. Notice the workers high up on the rock face to the left, presumably prying loose rock to create a stable edifice. *(Enid Nordlund Collection)*

addition, the American, Mackinaw, and Peabody mining companies were reportedly ready to resume work there. The Del Campo Mining Company already had a large crew at work on its Weden Creek/Gothic Basin properties, which added to the argument for reopening the line.

On May 8, 1913, talks took place in a conference room at the Commercial Club in Everett. Due to a miscommunication of dates, the State Railway Commission, which had asked for an order reestablishing the rail service, failed to appear. Still, Northern Pacific officials and an attorney for the plaintiffs met. The plaintiffs had filed separate complaints to the commission, and they decided to consolidate them into one case, to be called the Birney Case. At the meeting, the railroad agreed to spend $16,000 to reopen the line, and Birney agreed to undertake the job as a contractor at that figure.

During the conference, railroad general manager Reid argued that rebuilding the line would cost $40,000 to $50,000. But the plaintiff's attorney argued that Birney, who had engineered the original line and had participated in past reconstruction projects, had estimated the cost at around $8,000. Reid said that if the line could be reopened for $10,000, the railroad would put up no resistance. The attorney said that Birney would reopen the railroad for $10,000 and would secure a bond to ensure completion of the work.

Reid then announced that the tracks near Monte Cristo were still under 3 to 6 feet of snow. Since the plaintiffs had not been in the mountains to verify this and had no other way to determine the cost, the rest of the meeting was postponed until engineers for the parties involved could inspect the right-of-way. The railway commission members stated that, when snow conditions allowed, they would accompany the engineers to Monte Cristo. June 14 was set as the date for the next hearing. But before that date, Northern Pacific and the miners reached an agreement: The railroad agreed to rebuild the line on a temporary basis, but the work would not

The sinkhole just down the line from Silverton was an eternal nemesis for the railway. The trestle work had to be constantly re-aligned and repaired as the unstable ground slowly moved. Many attempts were made to stabilize the soil, but none worked. One proposal called for building wing dams to divert the Stillaguamish River to dry the soil, but this plan was never carried out. *(Enid Nordlund Collection)*

A pack train in 1912 before its arduous trek to the Del Campo Mine high above the banks of Weden Creek. This photo was taken at Weden Creek Station. Pictured here are, from the left: Elizabeth Kyes, James Kyes (foreman of the mine), Mrs. Banta, Elsie Banta, Jimmy Kyes, Leo Kyes, Velma Kyes, and two unidentified men. *(John A. Juleen photo)*

be sufficient for the operation of full-size trains. If the mines were to develop sufficiently to provide a paying proposition to the railroad at a later date, the railroad would rebuild the line for permanent operation.

In the meantime, Birney put in an order for a gas car—a motor car equipped with flanged wheels that could pull small cars behind it—to bring men and supplies to the mines above Silverton and lead to the reopening of those mines. These conveyances, which were used in railroad construction work, were known as "galloping gooses."

On June 19, 1913, a pile driver arrived over the tracks to Silverton for repairing road damage farther up the line. In mid-July, a train brought the Northern Pacific's track building tools and machinery to Monte Cristo. It was the first train to reach the terminus since 1909.

By the end of July, the five active mining companies at Monte Cristo employed 75 men, and the boomtown feel was again in the air. The railroad bed from Silverton to Monte Cristo was in better condition than expected, prompting visions that the line would be put in first-class shape for shipping ore to the smelter. But rail service was still limited to one equipment train a week. Once the gas car arrived, a second trip would be added.

On August 13, the train leaving Hartford was so badly overcrowded, with 135 passengers, that railroad agents had to borrow a tourist sleeper from a Canadian Pacific train.

Weden Creek Station, about 2¹/₂ miles below Monte Cristo. The near building is the Del Campo Mine warehouse, where goods were stored until the pack trains could carry them to the mine workings high above the Weden Creek Valley. *(Enid Nordlund Collection)*

This drew attention to earlier requests for better rail service along the Monte Cristo branch of the railroad. In addition, the train carried 26,000 pounds of freight. Most of the passengers were destined only for Silverton, which was considered, for all practical purposes, the upper terminus of the line. Those who wanted to travel beyond that point had to ride on one of two push cars pulled by horses or take an old motor car with flanged wheels that could hold 10 passengers and a bit of baggage. A motor-driven speeder that could hold either four passengers or about a half-ton of freight was also available.

Meanwhile, Birney's gas car was being built in Granite Falls using local parts because his original supplier in the east did not have a gas car in stock. More good news came from the Monte Cristo mines on October 10, 1913, when 35 tons of ore from the Ben Lomond Mine (the old Rainy Mine) passed

Lucky Owens, a local mine owner, on the platform of the Del Campo Mining Company's warehouse at Weden Creek Station on the Hartford Eastern Railway. After the goods were delivered by train and stored in the warehouse, they were transferred to pack trains for the trip to the mine high above the Weden Creek Valley. *(Enid Nordlund Collection)*

though Everett on its way to the smelter in Tacoma. This was taken to mean that the beginning of the imagined new boom at Monte Cristo was becoming a reality.

Restored Service to Monte Cristo

In January 1914, a work train and a large force of men repaired bridges and cleared the roadbed between Silverton and Monte Cristo. However, heavy snow along the line caused delays and completion of the work was not expected until late spring. In late January, a slide near the former tunnel #4 caused a temporary delay in rail traffic beyond Robe Canyon, cutting off supplies and transportation beyond that point. Work was halted until late April, when two large crews worked their way up the line toward Monte Cristo.

At Monte Cristo, miners from several different companies eagerly awaited the arrival of the first train of the year. One crew worked near Silverton, removing rock for riprapping the "pothole" where the Stillaguamish River had washed out a large cavern near the roadbed. This might have been the sinkhole just up the road from the present-day Youth on Ages trailhead. Another crew, equipped with a pile driver, worked near Monte Cristo, repairing bridges and the roadbed. By the end of May, the work was nearly done. One train carrying equipment for the Ben Lomond Mine had already crept gingerly over the tracks and into Monte Cristo a few days before, but the only other means of transportation was a gas car or speeder. This was welcome news, because the Ben Lomond Mine already had a score of cars at Monte Cristo loaded with ore, waiting for a locomotive to pull them out of the mountains and down to Tacoma for processing.

Development work was carried out at many of the Monte Cristo properties in 1914. Birney planned to extend the railroad's concentrator spur to the Rainy shaft of his (renamed) Ben Lomond Mine. Operations were somewhat hampered, however, due to an unstable roadbed between Silverton

A group enjoys a one-horsepower trip up the Monte Cristo line during one of the railroad's slack periods. This photo was probably taken in or near Silverton. The woman on the left side of the rear row might be the photographer's wife. *(Phil Woodhouse Collection, John A. Juleen photo)*

A Hartford Eastern utility gas car maneuvers a new log into place at Red Bridge for use as a piling to repair the flood-damaged railway. The Hartford Eastern Railway lacked the money to support the section gangs that had serviced the Everett and Monte Cristo; it relied on a small repair force to service the entire line. *(Enid Nordlund Collection)*

and Monte Cristo. Heavy cargo was delivered by the railroad to Silverton, then the merchandise had to be hauled into Monte Cristo on a variety of lightweight cars on the rails or by horse cart. The Northern Pacific ran only one train per week to Silverton. A new mining company at Monte Cristo, the Boston American, drove a tunnel from just above the town into the side of Toad Mountain toward Silver Lake. It hoped to strike the vein of the O&B Mine at depth, thus exposing an enormous body of gold ore. If this effort were to succeed, it would bode well for the railroad.

At last, on June 24, scheduled passenger trains began traveling from Everett all the way to Monte Cristo for the first time since 1908. A combination freight and passenger train made the trip every Wednesday.

The Moose Lodge of Snohomish made arrangements with the railroad for an excursion to Monte Cristo that would include a picnic and a live band on Sunday, July 26, 1914. Tickets sold quickly for what promised to be a relaxing day in the heart of the Cascades. However, the trip was canceled when the roadbed was found to be very tender and not sufficiently repaired for such heavy-duty use. Once-a-week ordinary traffic was just about the limit, and a heavily loaded passenger train was apparently more than the reconstructed roadbed could bear.

On December 16, 1914, the last scheduled train of the year left Everett for Monte Cristo, but the Northern Pacific announced that it would attempt to maintain service as far as Silverton throughout the winter. A number of hardy souls remained in Monte Cristo all winter.

Meanwhile, the mining companies, unable to ship ore, experienced problems. The Ben Lomond Mining Company fell into receivership over the winter, and prospects for shipping more ore were slim.

In the later years, Red Bridge was but a trestle where the railroad crossed the Stillaguamish River. The spring storms often took their toll as logs and branches in the river tore the underpinnings from the tracks. In this photo, a steam pile driver is in position to set a new bent of timber to support the weakened structure. *(Enid Nordlund Collection)*

The Hartford Eastern at Red Bridge often looked like this after storms and floods ravaged the area. According to Bob Thorsen, an eyewitness, a gas car was once run over the line when it was in this condition. This was a testament to the strength of the fishplates tying the rails together. *(Enid Nordlund Collection)*

A gas-powered touring car fitted with flanged wheels enters the eastern portal of tunnel #3 on its way to the towns of Granite Falls and Hartford. Probably taken during the Hartford Eastern days of the Monte Cristo line, this photo shows that a variety of equipment was used on the line. *(Enid Nordlund Collection)*

A group of berry pickers on their way to the fields. When the railroad was out of service or when locomotives didn't run, people used many innovative methods to transport people or goods up and down the line. This one-horse car did the job quite nicely on a late summer or early autumn day. *(Enid Nordlund Collection)*

In later years, Jimmy Mortenson lived at Goat Lake and transported supplies from Barlow Pass up to the camp below the lake. He is shown here in 1925 guiding a load of lumber up the trail toward the camp. *(University of Washington, Penn Mining Company Collection)*

With the great rotary plows moved off the Monte Cristo line years earlier, less efficient push plows cleared the tracks during the winter. The snow was often as deep as a locomotive was high, so the train would sometimes stall or the drivers would slip as the snow jammed against the plow blades. *(Enid Nordlund Collection)*

A Hartford Eastern gas car emerges from the western portal of tunnel #3 in Robe Canyon on its way down to Granite Falls and Hartford. This end of the tunnel was dug through soft earth and loose rock, as evidenced by the heavy shoring seen here. *(Phil Woodhouse Collection)*

5

The Timber Industry and the Railroad

*B*y the 1890s, industrial and agricultural development in the Puget Sound region was feeding demand for timber for buildings, barns, homes, bridges, and wharves. San Francisco's need for wood products also helped spur the growth of the Northwest forest industry. Logging operations and sawmills were already in operation from Everett to Granite Falls before the turn of the century, but the lack of a railroad kept the industry from developing rapidly. In 1892, a reporter riding on one of the first trains between Hartford and Granite Falls on the uncompleted Everett and Monte Cristo Railway described a canyon of tall trees in which one could see only a few feet beyond the right-of-way, with just a few sawmills and shingle mills dotting the line.

By 1905, mining along the line and especially in the Monte Cristo area had ground to a halt. However, by this time steam-powered logging equipment had enabled the logging companies to move inland from the waterways, and the areas surrounding the Everett and Monte Cristo Railway right-of-way contained vast tracts of timber. The existing railroad gave loggers access to these tracts, and the Northern Pacific Railway (later, the Rucker Brothers by way of a lease from the Northern Pacific) enjoyed profits from hauling logs out of the valley to the mills in Granite Falls and Everett.

Once the Everett and Monte Cristo line was in full operation, the vast expanse of forest east of Everett was quickly exploited. According to *Big Four Ice Caves: Hiking the Big Four Ice Caves Trail* by Harry Majors (Northwest Press, 1998), a sawmill operated at Perry Creek, a few miles above Silverton, in about 1895. The Everett and Monte Cristo might have built a sawmill there around 1893-94 to provide timber for building the railroad.

The Silverton Nursery

Between 1908 and 1916, the U.S. Forest Service operated the first public tree nursery in the Pacific Northwest at the Silverton Ranger Station just west of Silverton. Organized in 1908 as part of the Snoqualmie National Forest, the ranger district was a prime location for experimentation in how to replant areas burned by forest fires and also to see if imported eastern hardwood trees could be grown successfully in the West. The majority of seedlings grown were Douglas fir and Western white pine, as well as Western red cedar, Norway spruce, larch, and Western yellow pine; the hardwood experiment was unsuccessful.

Two men preparing a row for seeds. Note the board with the two levers, which they used to create a furrow. The workers hired to do the planting came from Seattle's "skid road" area. They were paid by the day and lived at a temporary camp at Buck Creek. *(U.S. Forest Service, Darrington Ranger District)*

The nursery was the brainchild of Burt Kirkland, forest supervisor, who later became a professor of forestry at the University of Washington. He and the district ranger, George Sawyer, were both fresh out of school and worked hard to develop this new endeavor.

The Everett and Monte Cristo Railway had caused major fires on nearby Long Mountain in 1897 as well as on Mount Dickerman west of Barlow Pass. Additional fires caused by the Northern Pacific had burned parts of the Green River Valley near Lester in King County. Now the railroad would bring in seed, supplies, and men to repair that damage and provide transportation out for the boxes of seedlings. All the seedlings were destined for burned and logged-over areas on U.S. Forest Service land. Commercial logging methods at the time had no provision for any replanting after harvesting timber.

In 1912 and 1913, the major plantings were completed. The 1913 planting was a 350-acre, 300,000-seedling Douglas Fir project on Granite Mountain near Rockdale. But the next year, a train bound for Monte Cristo started a fire at Mount Dickerman. A crew discovered the fire but raced down to Silverton for reinforcements instead of battling the blaze while it was small. By May 1915, the laborious task of replanting had been repeated.

Using a gauge board to plant seedlings. After one or two seasons, the seedlings were transplanted from the seedling beds to seedling orchards, where they matured for another year. The men in this photo are placing individual seedlings in notches in the board to ensure proper spacing. *(U.S. Forest Service, Darrington Ranger District)*

Seedlings destined for the Buck Creek burns of 1904 and 1914. Note the experimental containers used to hold the seedlings for transport. Each ventilated box contained damp moss to provide moisture. The seedlings were wrapped in bundles of 25, and each box held roughly 120 bundles. *(U.S. Forest Service, Darrington Ranger District)*

Seedlings were also shipped to burned areas in Oregon, notably the Mount Hood National Forest and the Tillamook area. Procedures for safely shipping the young seedlings were not yet established, so the nursery tried using wooden boxes built on-site and packing the seedlings in them along with wet moss collected from local trees. This proved unsuccessful because the moss did not retain enough moisture for the long train ride, and many seedlings perished.

Although almost a million seedlings were raised at the nursery, the facility was closed in 1916 because the major sites had been restored and the Forest Service decided to concentrate operations at a large-scale nursery at Wind River in southern Washington. Major slides in Robe Canyon in 1910 and 1915 and delays in shipping by rail also led to expensive losses when trees were sent to other areas. The existence, operation, and closure of the nursery were thus directly tied to the fortunes of the Monte Cristo branch of the Northern Pacific Railway.

District Ranger George Sawyer at the Silverton Ranger Station in 1909. Note the number of stars on the American flag. *(U.S. Forest Service, Darrington Ranger District)*

The Silverton Ranger Station during the time of the Hartford-Eastern. The station had been rebuilt with a simpler roof line that was probably much more practical for the winter snow. The small platform at left kept passengers dry as they waited for the railcar. *(U.S. Forest Service, Darrington Ranger District)*

The railroad, which ran between Silverton and the base of Mount Dickerman, required a large amount of timber for trestles. Perry Creek was a whistle stop in the 1894 and 1895 Everett and Monte Cristo timetables. A building of the Big Four Mining Company was also located at Perry Creek.

At the head of Robe Canyon, Truitt K. Robe, a local timber baron for whom the canyon was named, built his Canyon Lumber Company mill in 1892 on his homestead next to the railroad. By 1895 the town of Robe had a post office, a hotel, a general store, and 150 residents. In 1901, the Everett Cedar Lumber Company started a logging enterprise at Gold Basin several miles east of Verlot. From 1909 to about 1913, the operation was run by the Gold Basin Lumber and Shingle Mill Company and there were about 75 people living in the Gold Basin area.

By 1906, the Granite Falls area alone had nearly a dozen mills. The Robe & Menzel Mill, built in 1902, had a daily output of 30,000 to 40,000 feet of lumber and included a planing mill and lath factory.

Farther up the railroad line at Black Creek, on a former U.S. Forest Service tract of cedar, fir, and hemlock, was the Moose Shingle Mill, which had been moved from Bothell in 1913. Several owners tried but failed to make a profit on bucket staves, heading stock, and shingles. Two dams on Black Creek facilitated operation of the mill. One served as a storage dam and the other impounded a millpond. In 1917, the upper dam gave way, taking out the lower one and the railroad bridge below. The last buyer was allegedly tricked into buying the mill in 1919 after the two dams were hastily rebuilt. Just beyond the famous "Sinkhole" was Sawyer Camp, better known as the Tulalip Sawmill Lumber Camp, which was built by the Rucker brothers. On the railroad, the mill became known as the station stop of Weigle.

However, most logs were destined for the Everett area with its huge mill capacities and its rail and port connections. In 1909, the principal shingle mills in Everett produced some 80 million shingles, including C. A. Blackman & Company with 40 million shingles, Ferry-Baker Lumber Company with 28,164,000 shingles, and McWilliams and Henry with 9,993,000 shingles. In 1919, the principal sawmills in Everett produced nearly 200 million board feet of finished lumber, including Canyon Lumber Company with 70 million, Ferry-Baker Lumber Company with 45 million, Robinson Manufacturing Company with 35 million, and Walton Lumber Company with 30 million. Dozens of smaller mills in the area also produced lumber and shingles.

The mills depended on a continuous supply of logs from the dozens of logging companies along the line. The loggers worked under difficult and dangerous circumstances, relying on hand tools to fall and buck the giant trees and on draft animals and steam-powered equipment to transport the logs to the loading points. The men lived in camps that followed the timber.

Perhaps the best description of life in a logging camp appeared in the *Seattle Post-Intelligencer* on March 17, 1907. A reporter named Clara Iza Price rode on an empty log train returning to the woods from the paper mill at Lowell. The train consisted of flatcars, so she rode in the caboose. Her destination was the logging camp at Woodland Spur about $2^1/_2$ miles up the Monte Cristo branch of the Northern Pacific line from Hartford Junction.

The reporter described the caboose as stuffy, "with a prevailing odor of leather cushions, which according to tradition and the assertion of appearances, had done duty as coaches for traveling loggers in various stages of illness or intoxication for a long period." The forward compartment of the caboose was warmed by a coal-burning stove. She described the curtains in the caboose as "the curtains a woman would have draped back from the windows, but which were tied in the middle with a knot of masculine determination that couldn't come undone to the end of time." The train did a great amount of switching between the mill and the station before it finally headed over the Snohomish River swing bridge up the tracks toward Snohomish. There it switched to the northbound tracks of the Northern Pacific (formerly the Seattle Lake Shore and Eastern) and headed toward Hartford Junction.

The train passed many small ranch houses on land largely covered with tree stumps. Soon, all that was visible were trees, "the base of their trunks hidden with the jungle-like growth of the Washington forest which prevents the eye from penetrating a rod beyond the outer edge of the wall of spruces with blue green spines and suggestions of brown cones, the cedar's dark plumes, the hemlock and fir." At Hartford, the train switched to the Monte Cristo Branch and made its way toward Woodland Spur. Price imagined herself "puffing into camp with the sound of axes ringing on every side; the crash of falling trees echoing from the distance and drivers shouting as they urged overburdened cattle along the road." But the train stopped along a nondescript, level stretch of track, with only a few houses visible in the distance and no sign of a logging camp. The train was continuing on to Granite Falls and then to the loading point where it would obtain the wood for its trip back to the mill. Price had to leave the train and trudge a mile through the snow, up the spur, to the Woodland camp.

The camp, she noted, was a "collection of shacks...with the exception of the neat little cottages of Mr. E. J. Lane, manager, and Mr. George Rofe, bookkeeper." It consisted of "the commissariat, the store, fifty feet in length, the cook house and dining room, perhaps ten feet longer than the store and wide in proportion, the five bunk houses with accommodations each for twenty-five men, the meat house, oil house, blacksmith shop and stables. In addition to these buildings are tents and shacks where live the better class of men, who do not care to mix with the genus lumbermen of the bunkhouses. In addition to these are the cabins of a number of Scandinavian teamsters whose families are with them in camp."

Price said of the camp store: "It offers novelties...and these consist of red, green, plaid, and striped mackinaws, boots with soles like iron and laces like ropes, leather belts mistaken by us for parts of a horse's harness as the iron buckles seemed too heavy for men's wear.... In the hardware line the novelties consist of wicked looking double-headed axes, saws with teeth that might gnash, springboard irons, crow-bars, pickaxes and iron wedges of various makes, with a murderous looking array of iron-tipped peaveys. There is, as a matter of course, a grocery side which is perhaps of the greatest importance with between two and three hundred hungry men to feed." The store's books included such entries as "twenty-five tons of flour consumed by the men in camp during the year 1900." Rofe also assumed the role of medic. Because of the frequent injuries to workers, he kept "Vaseline in gallon cans, painkiller in two-gallon jugs, court plaster by the yard and absorbent cotton by the bale."

The camp's pay ledger showed many nationalities, "from Russian Finns, to Maoris from New Zealand, though perhaps Scandinavians predominate." Price found mealtime to be especially interesting: "In the dining room are five long tables with benches on either side. Plates for twenty men are laid at each table. The cutlery is substantial, the dishes solid and the provisions plentiful. The room is warmed by a great iron box set in sand and capable of swallowing half a dozen sticks of cordwood.... A huge roasting pan was filled with great chunks of beef—the very best cuts, for whole beeves hang in the meat house, and the head cook chooses for himself. Five gallon kettles of soup, of tomatoes and other vegetables were simmering on the range which filled one side of the shed. The young cook—Joe Reilly—who looked more like a soldier than a chef, was dipping up tapioca pudding with a shovel into dishes the size of individual tea trays, and in an enormous wash tub bread for the daily baking was rising."

An example of the huge trees in the valley and the men who cut them. This western red cedar is being bucked into 4-foot pieces to create shingle bolts. Note the notch in the foreground stump, which was used to hold the springboard that the logger would stand on to fall the giant tree with axe and saw. Springboards elevated the logger above the butt swell of the tree to get into straight-grained timber and reduce the amount of cut necessary to fall the tree. *(Everett Public Library Collection, G. W. Kirk photo)*

The day after Price arrived, work in the woods resumed. She noted 20-foot sleds drawn by teams of horses and workers who sang with magnificent voices. "Felling the trees gives them opportunity to display their great strength," she wrote, "which in some cases is accomplished by a certain native grace wasted on the wilderness. They stand on spring-boards whose irons are planted in the great trunks eight or ten feet from the ground, as the base of the trees are wind shaken and both difficult to split and useless for lumber."

A horse-drawn sled with a load of 4-foot shingle bolts destined for Best Shingle Company's mill #2 near Robe in 1906. One man holds a bucket of grease and a brush to grease the skid road logs to make the pull easier. The operator standing on the sled is Frank Davis. At the mill, each bolt was cut into three 16-inch pieces, then cut into thick slabs, and then sawn at a slight angle to created tapered shingles. The bridge shown here is a crib bridge made of un-marketable logs. Note the hand-split planks used as the bridge decking. *(Everett Public Library Collection, Darius Kinsey photo)*

The boys of the camp were usually employed as skid greasers. After the branches were removed, the trees were "bucked" into suitable lengths and dragged to camp on sleds for loading onto the railcars. They were hauled down a path "paved" by logs laid at intervals of 5 to 10 feet, which provided a bearing surface. To facilitate this process, the paving logs had to be greased periodically. "With a floppy rag at the end of a pole," Price wrote, "they go about dipping the rag in a can of crude petroleum and slapping it upon the skids or hewn logs that form beds for the sleds to slip along on. Great barrels of the disagreeable stuff stand at convenient distances along the roads leading to the wood piles, and the 'greasers' may be seen, when not at work, warming themselves by fires built at the side of a huge stump."

The Woodland camp cut about 900 cords of wood every week. The cutters were paid by the day, while the teamsters were paid by the cord. Most of the men spent their wages immediately on drinking and carousing in nearby towns. A few, however, were more

The Moose Shingle Company's mill on Black Creek near the Everett and Monte Cristo line. The dam enabled the water level to be raised to the bottom of the loading conveyor so that shake bolts could be brought up to the mill. *(U.S. Forest Service, Darrington Ranger District)*

prudent with their hard-earned wages. Two such young men in the camp spent their off hours studying. A chapter of the Northwest Lumberman's Evangelical Society set up in the camp to tend to the spiritual and educational needs of the men.

Trees were harvested first in the flatlands, and later in the foothills and mountains above. The Europeans who first set foot west of the Cascades in Washington State thought that there were so many trees, of such enormous size, that they could never all be cut down. But by the 1920s, the magnificent forests that had carpeted the western slopes of the Cascades were virtually gone. With the advent of mechanized logging, the forests seemed to melt away. Today, when you drive along State Route 92 to Granite Falls, keep in mind that all of the picture-postcard farmland around you was once thick forest towering hundreds of feet.

The Moose Shingle Company's mill. The powerhouse is under construction at the left. Note the pile of bricks for use around the boiler. *(U.S. Forest Service, Darrington Ranger District)*

(facing page) Finished shingles on a suspension bridge built by the Davis Shingle Company in 1906 near the Everett and Monte Cristo's tunnel #2. The mill operated until 1916. *(U.S. Forest Service, Darrington Ranger District)*

Getting the "big sticks" out of the woods. The trees were bucked to length and yarded to the railroad loading area. The photo shows the steam donkey, which pulled the logs to this point, lining up the logs—probably for yarding by the next donkey down the line. *(Everett Public Library Collection, G. W. Kirk photo)*

The parbuckling method of loading logs. Behind the boy is the skid road over which the steam donkey engine pulled in cut logs. After a log was yarded in, one of the donkey's cables was looped through the pulleys to roll the log up the ramp and onto the waiting flatcar (visible on the right). As each flat car was filled, the train was moved forward to bring the next empty flatcar into place. *(Everett Public Library Collection, G. W. Kirk photo)*

Yarding and loading logs deep in the woods. The flatcar in the foreground is loaded and ready to go, and the car behind it is being loaded. Behind it, barely visible on the right edge of the photo, are more empty flat cars. The steam donkey in the center is doing double duty, both yarding the logs in for loading and loading the logs using the cable suspended from the block at the top of the spar tree. Note the unusually large number of guy lines to the right of the spar pole to provide support. *(Everett Public Library Collection, G. W. Kirk photo)*

(facing page) A loading area near Weden Creek. Note the use of two steam donkeys, one (partially visible on the right) to yard the logs and another (in the center) for loading. This method of loading employed a spreader bar and two separate cables with grappling hooks. Each log was lifted and then lowered onto the waiting flatcar. This method was dangerous; the grappling hooks were later replaced by tongs or chokers for a more secure hold on the log. *(Enid Nordlund Collection)*

The 150-foot Howe truss bridge that carried the Johnson-Dean spur from the Monte Cristo line at Cutoff to the logging company's base camp. *(Bockmeier Collection)*

The Johnson-Dean base camp up the track from the junction at Cutoff on the Monte Cristo line. The family housing is at the rear; the large building on the right in the front is the dormitory. The other buildings in the front include the office and the company store. *(Bockmeier Collection)*

(facing page, top) A camp train parked on the Wheeler-Osgood logging spur just outside tunnel #2. The cars were connected to enable people to go between them in inclement weather. The two ladies in the doorway are cooks. Visible on the tracks in the foreground is a velocipede—the railroad equivalent of a bicycle. *(Enid Nordlund Collection)*

(facing page, bottom) The sawmill at the lower tunnel of the Del Campo Mine on Weden Creek around 1912. Notice the cut timbers protruding from the left side of the enclosure. Having a sawmill at the mine reduced the effort and expense of hauling timber over the railroad and then toting it up the steep trail. The lack of a boiler and a smokestack probably meant that the sawmill got its power from the mine's waterwheel power plant. *(John A. Juleen photo)*

A lumber mill crew with railroad ties. This style of tie was known as a slabbed tie because only the top and bottom of the log were cut flat. Small-diameter logs were often used to make ties because they were otherwise unmarketable. *(U.S. Forest Service, Darrington Ranger District)*

Workers at the Monte Cristo sawmill in the 1890s. The machinery for the mill was hauled over a puncheon road from Sauk City (Rockport) after being delivered there by steamboat up the Skagit River. The mill was in operation before the railroad reached Monte Cristo. Local merchants were disappointed to learn that the mill, owned by the mining companies, produced timbers exclusively for the mines. Once the railroad was completed into Monte Cristo in 1893, lumber could be shipped in from Everett. The mill was eventually converted to the Monte Cristo railway station. The locomotive to the left of the building is blurred because of the long shutter speeds required at the time. *(U.S. Forest Service, Darrington Ranger District)*

The Blackman brothers' mill in Snohomish in 1892. Despite the many fire barrels along the roof, this mill eventually burned to the ground. The man in the foreground wearing a hat and holding a stick is the bullpuncher, who drove the ox teams. All of the ox teams are paired with yokes; the six oxen on the right are chained together to form a team. Visible in the left foreground are horse-drawn wagons that transported the finished lumber. *(Everett Public Library Collection)*

The Canyon Lumber Company's mill at Robe after it had been bought by the Johnson-Dean Company. The Canyon Lumber Company moved to Everett because the railroad refused to allow it to ship long timbers through Robe Canyon. The railroad required that all products fit into a boxcar. This froze the lumber company out of the long timber market. Johnson-Dean was apparently satisfied with boxcar-sized products. *(Enid Nordlund Collection)*

6

The Hartford Eastern

O n May 11, 1915, the Rucker brothers, who ran a large lumber mill in the town of Lake Stevens, signed a 10-year lease at $15,000 per year with the Northern Pacific to use the Monte Cristo Branch of the Northern Pacific in their extensive logging operations above Granite Falls. They became the general common carrier in passenger and freight, and the railroad was renamed the Hartford Eastern Railway Company. This seemed like an ideal solution for the Northern Pacific, which had wanted to divest itself of the troublesome and unproductive branch line for some time.

The lease took effect on June 1, 1915. The Hartford Eastern maintained daily service from Hartford to Silverton, and on Wednesdays the train ran all the way to Monte Cristo. The Ruckers leased only the trackage from Hartford to Monte Cristo, hence the name Hartford Eastern.

All the passengers were carried by regular gas cars refitted for rail service, thus eliminating the big heavy steam locomotives. On August 28, 1915, the first of the Ruckers' gas cars appeared in Everett and caused quite a stir. It was built by the White Motor Truck Factory and was a 1.5-ton vehicle with solid rubber tires, which were to be replaced with regular, spoke artillery wheels fitted with metal flanged tires. The truck was painted all white, had a covered top and broad comfortable seats for up to 22 passengers, and was equipped with a

A privy at Monte Cristo with a Northern Pacific ticket office sign attached as a joke. This photo was taken in 1929, long after the Northern Pacific stopped rail traffic to Monte Cristo. *(Dorothy VanNorman photo)*

A galloping goose viewed through tunnel #5 in Robe Canyon. This photo was taken between 1915 and 1920, during the halcyon days of the Hartford Eastern Railway when tourists traveled in large numbers along the line. *(Granite Falls Historical Society Collection)*

30-horsepower engine. It could travel up to 40 miles per hour. The second gas car was built in Seattle. It was similar to an interurban car but a little shorter. Both cars had a regulation 56-inch tread. A third car for the Hartford Eastern line, also built in Seattle, was a gasoline-powered combination passenger, baggage, and mail carrier of the interurban design equipped with fenders similar to those of big electric locomotives. It was driven by a 50-horsepower gas engine with a double chain connected to a single set of rear-drive wheels. It was 30 feet long and 9 feet wide and could accommodate 30 passengers as well as 2 tons of baggage.

More Winter Problems

The snows of early 1916 created such havoc in the region that no trains ran through the mountains and mail had to be carried in on foot. It was said to be the worst snowfall since 1893. Barns and houses collapsed under the weight of the snow, even in the low elevations of the Snohomish River Valley. Snowplows that normally kept the mountain passes open were moved to the lowlands to keep the rail lines along the Puget Sound open, leaving mountain communities isolated.

Residents of Silverton began to complain that the Rucker brothers were not doing enough to keep the line open. Supplies were not coming into the town. President Pritchard of the Hartford Eastern explained that this was the company's first experience running a railroad during the winter and that it simply didn't have enough equipment to clear the line. He said that the tracks would be cleared as soon as weather conditions permitted and that the next winter they would have more snow removal equipment.

Just when the tracks were finally opened is not clear. More heavy snow was reported in Everett and the mountains in early March. On June 18, 1916, about 200 visiting bankers boarded a special train at Lake Stevens for an excursion to Monte Cristo. The weather was clear and very hot, and spectacular waterfalls and the raging Stillaguamish and Sauk

(facing page) Gas car #23 of the Hartford Eastern approaches the eastern portal of tunnel #1 as it leaves Robe Canyon. The first half of this tunnel was bored through solid rock, but the western half was in soft soil and loose rock. The supporting beams caught fire several times and caused the collapse of the western portion of the tunnel. The fires were usually caused by sparks from a locomotive. Once steam locomotives no longer traversed the rails, the threat of fire was greatly reduced. *(Enid Nordlund Collection; photographer unknown, but possibly John A. Juleen)*

A gas car being delivered to or picked up from Hartford Junction. The car might have been in town for an overhaul or other repairs, or it might have been delivered to the rails to begin service for the first time. This photo shows how light and small most of the gas cars were. *(Enid Nordlund Collection)*

rivers added to the view. The train consisted of a regular locomotive pulling two flat cars, on which were mounted comfortable seats. The open cars were resplendent with flowers from the Ruckers' garden. A caboose followed the whole ensemble. Everett resident "Punk" Healy brought along his megaphone and called attention to points of interest. At Barlow Pass, one of the cars managed to jump the tracks, causing a slight delay. In the meantime, lunch was served, which included ice cream and a refreshing drink from an ice-cold stream. At Monte Cristo, the tourists walked around and enjoyed the magnificent

Safety First

Grover McDowell, the mail carrier along the railroad, was hauled into court in October 1916 and pleaded guilty to trespassing on the property of the Hartford Eastern. McDowell used a speeder to transport the mail along his route, and this was said to endanger not only himself but also the lives and property of those on the regular trains. He argued that this had been common practice in the past, even when the railroad was run by the Northern Pacific. The railroad argued that after the complaint was filed, an accident had occurred with another speeder on the railroad, and that other accidents could certainly happen along the sharp curves on the line. McDowell was found guilty and was ordered to pay a $1 fine and costs amounting to $10.55.

view. The return trip was even more delightful in the cooler air. The only problem on the return trip was when a photographer lost his new Panama hat and insisted that the train stop so he could retrieve it.

In June 1916, the Hartford Eastern purchased a 2-ton truck from the Paddock-Fowler Auto Company. The truck was built by the Signal Company and was equipped for passenger service on the rail line. It had a high-powered engine that ran on distillate (gasoline) and could carry 30 passengers. It complemented the White car between Hartford and Monte Cristo.

On August 2, a rockslide in the canyon at tunnel #3 blocked the line for several days. On October 30, another rock and earth slide came down the side of the Robe Canyon at the western portal of tunnel #3, completely burying the tracks. This slide was in the same area as the August slide, but much worse. Until the blockage was removed, traffic was rerouted over the old Johnson-Dean logging road above the slide area.

By Christmas, Monte Cristo was cut off from the world by 35 miles of snowdrifts, which left it nearly a ghost town again after many hardy souls marched out on snowshoes.

During the winter, the many waterfalls along the Hartford Eastern line, especially those in Robe Canyon, turned into fantasies of ice. In this photo, gas car #22 stops to let passengers take in the splendor. *(Enid Nordlund Collection)*

World War I

When the United States entered the First World War, all available materials and personnel were poured into the effort. Many men felt it was their patriotic duty to join the military. It became impossible to obtain explosives for anything except the war effort. Casual labor vanished, and many mining companies had to close because they could no long hire miners or obtain material for their mines. The Boston American Mining Company at Monte Cristo fell victim to these shortages, suspending operations for the duration of the war.

Perhaps the only thing worse than trying to drive a gas car up snow-covered tracks was trying to drive it through a snowstorm in progress. Here the driver attends to the unpleasant task of removing packed snow from Hartford Eastern gas car #22. *(Enid Nordlund Collection)*

Keeping the Line Open

In January 1917, the Hartford Eastern was brought before the State Public Service Commission to answer a complaint filed by the Mackie Mill Company of Gold Basin, R. H. Buchanan of Robe, J. O. Kjelsburg of Silverton, and the Boston American Mining Company of Monte Cristo. The complaint alleged that the railway failed to make proper efforts to keep the line open and free of slides, and that it had failed to use a steam shovel and an adequate number of men to keep the tracks cleared. It also stated that tunnel #3 was afflicted by "chronic slides of loose rock and mud" at its portals. The complainants also asked that the railroad be compelled to construct a trail over the top of the tunnel to provide a means of transporting passengers and freight when the tunnel was impassable.

The railroad denied that it lacked diligence and argued that it had used every reasonable means considering the mountainous terrain and the difficulty of winter maintenance. It said that the methods requested by the complainants were too expensive to be justified by the meager amount of business in such a sparsely settled area. The commission agreed with the company and stated that no further action was necessary. However, Judge W. P. Bell, the attorney for the railroad, announced that a shed would be built over the tracks at one end of the tunnel that had been turned into an open cut. In May, the Public Service Commission ordered the railroad to notify it whenever the line was impassable and ordered the company to maintain a register book at all stations along the line.

(facing page) After the big rotary plows were removed from the line, the Hartford Eastern used this small rotary. Pushed ahead of one of the gas cars, this little plow could hold its own in moderate snow. Here it is parked at its staging area in Silverton. The Brower House, also known as the "tin house" because of its metal roof, is in the background. Behind the Brower House is Long Mountain. *(Bob Thorsen Collection)*

In December, the highest water ever recorded washed though the canyons. Heavy damage was reported along the Hartford Eastern. January 1919 brought more heavy rains and flood damage along the line. In early March, a large slide blocked the tracks near tunnel #1. It was about 100 feet deep and 175 feet wide. Nearly 300 feet of track had been washed into the river. The Rucker brothers ingeniously set up a hydraulic sluicing operation by diverting water into a sluice that carried it from above the canyon to wash the dirt and debris away. In addition, they moved a large fire pump from their mill at Lake Stevens to the slide-damaged tunnel. With the boiler of a large locomotive providing steam to run the pump, workers directed the water spray at the blockage through monitor nozzles, and the tunnel was cleared and ready for traffic by the end of March.

Competition from the Automobile

Twentieth-century progress was catching up with the remote country east of Granite Falls by 1919, when a dirt motorcar road stretched around Robe Canyon all the way to the base of Mount Pilchuck. This could not have been good news for the little Hartford Eastern

The Hartford Eastern's small rotary plow in action. Although not as mighty as the Leslie-pattern rotary plows of the Everett and Monte Cristo days, this little unit could make reasonable headway against light to moderate snow and was usually used between Silverton (where it was based) and the Big Four Inn. *(Enid Nordlund Collection)*

The Inn at Big Four

The Rucker brothers' new Big Four Inn (formerly Camp Glacier) opened to the public on July 2, 1921. It was a large, three-story building with 50 rooms, hot and cold water in the bathrooms, a large magnificent fireplace, and a spectacular view of the surrounding snow-capped peaks. It soon became a popular year-round resort. It sported its own power plant for the electric lights in the building. The tailrace of the plant was diverted into a man-made lake named Crystal Lake, which served as a reflecting pond for the inn. The inn added to the Rucker brothers' profits from their logging operations along the upper Stillaguamish River.

Railway, which relied on tourist traffic to supplement its logging and freight business. But progress was progress. To offset this, the Rucker brothers began building a resort at Camp Glacier (which later became the Big Four Inn) with cabins and tents for guests. Hotels at

The ice and snow on the Hartford Eastern were often too much for the lightweight gas cars, even though they had flangers. The ice and compact snow caused derailments such as the one pictured here. When this happened, it was everyone to the shovels, and the car had to be manually rerailed (presumably with the aid of a rerailer). *(Enid Nordlund Collection)*

Silverton and the Cascrest Inn at Monte Cristo also provided lodging for travelers. With World War I over, the Boston American Mining Company at Monte Cristo prepared for full-scale mining activity since men, powder, and machinery were again available.

To add to the bad news for the Rucker brothers, their big mill at Lake Stevens burned to the ground in late May 1920. So intense was the fire that the mill was completely destroyed in a half-hour. A locomotive parked on a trestle over a portion of Lake Stevens rolled into the water as the wooden structure burned. It still rests on the bottom of the lake, under 35 feet of water and 14 feet of mud.

In 1920, an avalanche destroyed the headhouse of the Boston American Mine, thus ending efforts to locate the ore beneath Toad Mountain.

New Owners

From 1922 to 1925, the valley went about its business with little fanfare. But the future didn't look bright for the Hartford Eastern. The Boston American Mine closed, and auto traffic threatened passenger and freight profits on the line. In 1925, the Rucker brothers' 10-year lease was to expire. They wanted to renew it, but the Northern Pacific wanted no further involvement in this small, nearly obsolete line. The Northern Pacific offered them only one option: Buy the railroad, stock and all, or forget the whole thing. With their Inn at Big Four and logging contracts on the Stillaguamish at stake, the Ruckers had little choice but to purchase the rail line. Thus, the Hartford Eastern bought the Northern Pacific branch line between Hartford Junction and Monte Cristo in October. The selling price was said to be $150,000, including a $50,000 mortgage to the Northern Pacific from the Hartford Eastern. According to the county assessor's office, the value of the line had been assessed at $537,000. For the next three and a half years, the Ruckers continued to carry passengers, freight, and mail, as well as logs and finished lumber from mills along the line.

A Real Power Play

In 1917, with the Everett region growing rapidly, the demand for electrical power was neccessary. To address the demand, the local power and light company was busily assessing rivers to determine which could be dammed. By this time, the torrents that rushed through Robe Canyon were legendary, and the canyon seemed a likely place for a dam and powerhouse. Plans were made to dam the South Fork of the Stillaguamish at tunnel #6 and plug the tunnel. The canyon was at its narrowest there, and the dam could be tall and not very wide. The rock in this area of the canyon was some of the firmest to be found and would likely withstand the pressure created by a dam. To prevent the lake from spilling out to the north of the Verlot area, a broad earthen dam would be built to prevent the lake from exiting.

The powerhouse was to be located just above Granite Falls on the river below the first crossing of the Hartford Eastern. To connect the dam and powerhouse, large penstocks (water supply pipes) were to be blasted through the solid rock between the two structures.

The plans included the rerouting of the Hartford Eastern tracks between Gold Basin and Granite Falls to keep them above the high-water level of the lake. The roads in the area were also to be rerouted. For whatever reason, the plans were shelved and never reconsidered. Perhaps the advent of World War I stopped the project. If the dam had been constructed, the Verlot Valley would be a very different place today.

In 1926, the Hartford Eastern began to operate at a deficit. By late 1928, this amounted to a total deficit of $139,803. The number of passengers was dwindling, and the line was sinking further into the red. In October 1929, the stock market collapse sent the nation into a depression that would last until just before World War II. With the nation's industries in a shambles and the logging industry already in a heavy slump, the Ruckers seized the opportunity to get out of the business and move on.

In March 1929, the Puget Sound Pulp and Timber Company took an option on the Rucker brothers' properties. On April 1, they exercised that option for a reported $575,000. The sale included the rebuilt mill at Lake Stevens, the Hartford Eastern Railway, the Inn at Big Four, and 4,500 acres of timberland. The inn was subsequently leased to A. J. Barnes, a well-known hotel operator from California. The railway also purchased a 43-foot, 40-passenger gas coach to supplement and largely supplant its existing passenger carriers. That summer, train service ran twice a day to the inn and the Monte Cristo area.

Abandonment

On April 28, 1933, the Interstate Commerce Commission signed an abandonment order for the Hartford Eastern. The

The flangers fitted to this gas car on the Hartford Eastern are visible above each rail. The snow packed on the windshield had to be manually removed before much progress could be made. This wet, heavy snow is typical of the Cascade foothills. *(Enid Nordlund Collection)*

railroad did not have to close down, but it was relieved of its common carrier obligations, which had required it to offer passenger and freight service. The I.C.C. had concluded that the railway was a money loser. The increased competition from roads, trucks, and motorcars, coupled with the Depression and the terrible condition of the railroad's right-of-way, had put the Hartford Eastern deep in the red. The abandonment affected all areas east of Verlot, including Silverton and the Inn at Big Four. Soundview Pulp Company, which had recently obtained title to the railroad, resort, and other holdings of the Puget Sound Pulp and Timber Company, could still use the railway to haul logs from U.S. Forest Service lands in the upper Stillaguamish region.

Some saw the abandonment as an excuse for the railroad to pull up the tracks along the affected section to make way for an auto road. Residents along the line were ready to fight. The Stillaguamish-Sauk Valley Association, after examining copies of the order, found only wording to permit cessation of operation "as to interstate and foreign commerce." They contended that for years the road had handled only intrastate commerce. Therefore, they reasoned that the commission's order did not affect the railroad's obligation to continue local traffic. They further concluded that the line was not under the jurisdiction of the I.C.C. except by legal technicality, since the Northern Pacific was no longer the owner. The association also pointed out that if the rail line above Verlot were to be

Hartford Eastern gas car #22 at the Inn at Big Four. The railroad between Hartford and Monte Cristo was often covered with enormous amounts of snow, especially above Silverton and on into Monte Cristo. As much as 15 feet of snow fell at Monte Cristo, and up to 8 feet at the inn. *(John A. Juleen photo)*

abandoned, the right-of-way would revert back to the owners of the adjoining properties, which for most of the distance was the U.S. government. They figured that this precluded use of the line as an auto road.

In September 1933, the Inn at Big Four and all of its water and electrical works, cabins, tents, and grounds were bought by U. M. Dickey, a former officer of the Hartford Eastern Company.

The Hartford Eastern tracks were plowed as far as the Inn at Big Four. Often the upper end of the line was closed during the winter. There was no way to turn the gas car around in deep snow, so the car had to back down to Silverton and be turned on a small turntable there. This view is from the opposite direction of the previous photo. *(John A. Juleen photo)*

The big turntable at Monte Cristo was not the only one on the line. The small frame device in this photo, partially hidden by snow, is the turntable at Silverton. A similar turntable was located at Hartford. Both were used to turn around the little gas cars. *(Bob Thorsen Collection)*

The driver of this gas car didn't see a log on the tracks until it was too late. The car was seriously smashed and derailed. The steam plume from a locomotive that was dispatched to help clear the wreck is visible above the roof of the car. *(Enid Nordlund Collection)*

On June 1, 1934, the assessed values of the Hartford Eastern Railway for 1933 and 1934 were reported by the state tax commission. For 1933 it was valued at $70,000, and for 1934 it was valued at only $25,000.

Persistent rains during the summer of 1934 damaged the right-of-way between Verlot and Silverton so badly that gas car traffic on the road was abandoned. Temporary repairs kept the line open to allow for speeder service to keep the inhabitants upstream supplied, but service was sometimes suspended because of the rising Stillaguamish River, which threatened the crossing at Red Bridge.

Another nail was driven in the coffin of the Hartford Eastern on July 6, 1934, when the *Everett Herald* reported that residents would have the opportunity to view progress on the new Mountain Loop Highway. Dedication of the modern steel bridge over the South Fork of the Stillaguamish just east of Granite Falls was set for July 17. The ceremonies were to be sponsored by the Granite Falls, Arlington, and Snohomish County chambers of commerce.

Information is sketchy about the railroad from 1934 to 1936, and only a few old-timers still remember details about its use during this period. Most of the trestles and bridges were apparently in poor condition, and extra care was taken by all traffic for fear that the next bridge would be gone when they got there or would collapse under the weight of a gas car. Time and use had taken their toll on the road-bed and bridges. The country was still in the grip of a depression. Demand for timber and mineral resources was low, and tourism had dwindled with the rest of the economy.

Because only a few dozen people re-mained above Verlot, expensive repairs to the railroad would have been a losing proposition. The line decayed to the point of abandonment as the modern highway made its way up the valley. In many places above Verlot, the high-way made use of the abandoned railroad right-of-way. In 1936, the rails were removed and shipped to Japan for scrap, thus ending forever one of the biggest railroad blunders in North-west history.

Gone were the popular excursion trains with their open-air cars and brass bands, and gone were the brief stops that allowed photog-raphers to jump off and get a shot of the train and the surrounding scenery. The faithful

This photo of a gas speeder on the Hartford Eastern line shows the weakened condition of the railroad in its later years. Enough maintenance was done to allow the structures to support the lighter gas cars. A steam locomotive would have plunged through such a lightly built trestle. *(Enid Nordlund Collection)*

"Galloping Goose" would no longer ply the rails, bringing food and mail to the hardy folk living above Old Robe. Gone, too, were the big weekend dances at the Inn at Big Four. And never again would a slightly inebriated guest at the Big Four yell, "Look out! Here comes the Black Mariah!" as Wyatt Rucker's big black Mitchell gas car neared the inn.

A gas car trailer loaded with rubbish at Monte Cristo. This material was regularly hauled to a local dump. *(Enid Nordlund Collection)*

A work train with a trailer on the turntable at Monte Cristo. *(Enid Nordlund Collection)*

Looking past the corner of the Inn at Big Four. The gas car, toting a passenger trailer, appears to have just arrived from Monte Cristo. The inn was popular until the Great Depression made it difficult for most people to travel. *(Enid Nordlund Collection)*

Two gas cars, a utility trailer, and the little rotary snowplow of the Hartford Eastern rest on a siding in Silverton. The Brower house is just above the siding in this summer scene. The slopes of Long Mountain form the backdrop. *(Bob Thorsen Collection)*

(facing page) As the Hartford Eastern line aged and as revenues diminished, the lack of maintenance was reflected in the wavy alignment of the rails, as shown in this photo. The added obstacle of the tree didn't help, either. Without heavy equipment, the removal of such roadblocks was a heavy-duty manual task. *(Enid Nordlund Collection)*

Epilogue: The Everett and Monte Cristo Railroad Today

As early as 1973, residents of King and Snohomish Counties became interested in preserving and displaying the historical sites along the old railroad right-of-way. A group of Boy Scouts built a trail though Robe Canyon that was kept open to the public by the grace and goodwill of the property owners, Scott Paper Company. The land was later acquired by Hancock Timber Resources, and finally sold to the Snohomish County Parks and Recreation Department, which worked with individuals, community groups, and government departments enabling public enjoyment of the rugged and beautiful canyon for future generations.

By 1999, the purchase of the property was complete. You can now hike from the trailhead on the eastern edge of Sand Hill (along the Mountain Loop Highway) all the way down though tunnels #6 and five, and if trail conditions permit, all the way to the eastern portal of tunnel #3. (The same problems exist today in the canyon—washouts and erosion.) A trail from the western portion of the property is expected to be completed sometime in 2000 or 2001, which will take the hiker down to the old lime kilns west of the first crossing of the Stillaguamish River near Cutoff.

To get to the trailhead that leads to the Robe Canyon tunnels, drive 7 miles east of Granite Falls on the Mountain Loop Highway. Park off the road on the south side of the highway just across from the Tupso Pass Road (Green Mountain Road), and begin your hike at the brick monument at the trailhead. Once the trail to the lime kilns is complete, the trailhead will be accessed from the Granite Falls area.

(following page) A hard-hatted worker walks across the timber trestle along the main line into Monte Cristo in 1919. The Boston-American Mining Company was the primary user of the Hartford Eastern Railway at this time. The disintegrating trestle on the left once carried traffic to and from the United Concentration Company's facility farther up the valley. The Boston-American concentrator is the prominent structure just to the right of center. It never processed any ore. *(Enid Nordlund Collection)*

A young Carvel Norton poses on the concentrator switchback spur at Monte Cristo. The continuation of the spur, after a switchback, is the trestle that appears upstream. Wilmans Peak hides its head in the clouds, which reveal the statuesque Count of Monte Cristo rock in the upper right. Taken from the trestle that carried the Hartford Eastern's main line into town, this photo, probably taken in the 1920s, shows the town in a state of decay as the winter snows take their toll. *(Enid Nordlund Collection)*

As an experiment, a herd of elk was introduced in the Verlot Valley above Robe Canyon. But the animals had been raised in close proximity to humans and would venture down to the tracks of the Hartford Eastern, where passengers would feed them. Then came hunting season. The elk were totally wiped out, and the experiment was deemed a failure. *(Enid Nordlund Collection)*

A Robe Stage car, which ran passengers, light freight, and mail up the Stillaguamish Valley between Snohomish, Lochsloy, Granite Falls, and Robe. As Americans relied more and more on the motorcar, the railroad's dominance waned and an increasing number of automobile roads were driven into the mountain communities along the Monte Cristo line. *(Phil Woodhouse Collection)*

A Robe Stage car at Lochsloy on the way to Granite Falls and Robe. The hood served as a convenient place to carry mailbags and other bulk cargo up the rough, new roads that were gradually replacing the railroad. Lochsloy still exists—it is the first gas station that you come to after leaving State Route 9 and heading toward Granite Falls. *(Phil Woodhouse Collection)*

The motor stage prepares to leave Hartford Junction for Granite Falls. The rails in the foreground carried rail traffic, while the new roads, which were built after lobbying by the Good Roads Association (later the American Automobile Association), carried the automobiles. *(Phil Woodhouse Collection)*

A group of passengers in front of the new Hartford Eastern gas car #100 at Hartford Junction. This car was patterned after the many interurban cars that were transportation mainstays in the United States in the 1920s and 1930s. It carried passengers as well as freight and mail (in the windowless area to the right). The car was powered by a 68-horsepower gasoline engine on one of the trucks. Unfortunately, the engine couldn't propel the steel car up the grades of the line without overheating or stalling. It was soon retired from service and was eventually sold. *(Enid Nordlund Collection)*

Gas car #100 at the Inn at Big Four. *(Enid Nordlund Collection)*

Gas car #22, one of the "galloping gooses" (geese?) that plied the Hartford Eastern Railway between Hartford and Monte Cristo from 1915 to the early 1930s. Like most of its kin, this one was a bus fitted with flanged wheels. The trailer hitched to the car allowed passengers to take in the mountain air. *(John A. Juleen photo)*

Gas car #100 approaching the Inn at Big Four from Monte Cristo. The building in the distance just left of the car is the inn's powerhouse, where a Pelton Wheel spun a generator that provided electric power to the mountain resort. The cabins on the left were part of the inn and were rented to visitors. Mount Dickerman is the prominent mass on the left, while some of the mountains near Monte Cristo are immediately above the car. *(John A. Juleen photo)*

Looking West at Big A Inn

Martin Johnson, a gas car driver, handyman, and photographer, tends the lawn in front of the Inn at Big Four. Hartford Eastern gas car #23 sits ready for the trip down the tracks. Snow on Long Mountain near Silverton is visible in the distance. *(John A. Juleen photo)*

The Inn at Big Four during the late 1920s or early 1930s. A gas car approaches from Silverton on its daily run. The inn is on the left, with some of its ancillary cabins across the tracks. On the right is the edge of Crystal Lake, a pond that was created by damming the tailrace of the inn's hydropower plant. *(John A. Juleen photo)*

In this 1921 photo, the Monte Cristo stage meets the "galloping goose" at the town of Hartford. The Inn at Big Four had just opened along the Hartford Eastern tracks above Silverton. Gas car #22 is laden with passengers, and baggage is being loaded into the bins under the seats. A trailer appears to be loaded with construction materials (and workmen). The gas car sports a 100-horsepower gas engine as its prime mover. *(Enid Nordlund Collection)*

(facing page) In September 1927, Fred Cleator of the U. S. Forest Service snapped this photo of Hartford Eastern gas car #22 on the rails near Silverton. The fellow posing with the car is probably the driver. *(U.S. Forest Service, Darrington Ranger District)*

One of the makeshift gas speeders that took over on the Hartford Eastern line when other forms of transport failed. This was a popular mode of travel, especially between Silverton and the Inn at Big Four in later years. Silverton residents often used the speeders to travel the few miles up the tracks to attend dances at the inn. Once, as one of the speeders was ready to depart for a dance, a local resident named Charlie Weischadel, who sported a full beard, tried to tag along. The younger fellows of the group decided that they didn't want him along, so they overpowered Charlie and clamped his whiskers in a set of switch points. Poor Charlie was stuck, tied to the rails by his beard, as the rest of the party faded up the line toward the inn. *(Enid Nordlund collection; photographer unknown—or did Charlie have a camera on him while he was clamped to the tracks?)*

Another makeshift gas speeder used on the Hartford Eastern line when the regular gas cars weren't running. Here, the car prepares to head down the line from Monte Cristo, where this photo was taken. *(Ellie Osbourne Collection)*

(facing page) By 1927, much of the town of Monte Cristo had succumbed to the winter weather. One of the few remaining buildings was the old Royal Hotel, with Wilmans Peak rising beyond. The rails could not carry steam locomotives by this time because they were maintained only to support the gas cars that now dominated the Hartford Eastern line. *(Enid Nordlund Collection)*

During its waning years in the late 1920s and early 1930s, the railroad often had little or no regular rail service. As a result, local entrepreneurs conjured up all manner of homespun devices. Most, such as this rig, made the trip only between Silverton and the Inn at Big Four. One reason was the popular weekly dance at the inn, which featured live music. *(Enid Nordlund Collection)*

A small gas speeder with rider sits on the Hartford Eastern tracks next to the Silverton depot. Stillaguamish Peak forms the backdrop on a splendid summer day. Notice the grass that engulfs the right-of-way. This was probably taken in the final years of the line. *(Phil Woodhouse Collection)*

In the 1920s, the old water tower at Monte Cristo sits forlornly beneath the peaks from which gold and silver had been wrested. The gas cars had no need for the water that was so critical to the steam locomotives of earlier years. *(Enid Nordlund Collection)*

Monte Cristo viewed from the South Fork of the Sauk River. This photo probably dates from the 1930s. The remains of the railroad trestle cross the river. The major buildings are, from the left: The Royal Hotel, the Riddle house, and the concentrator of the Boston American Mining Company rising above the company's headquarters/cookhouse. *(Enid Nordlund Collection)*

The Black Mariah, Wyatt Rucker's personal railcar. *(Pemco Webster & Stevens Collection, Museum of History and Industry)*

A Driving Tour:
Hartford to Barlow Pass

Highway 92 follows roughly the same route as the railroad, and a drive along this road will give you a very good sense of what a ride out to Monte Cristo would have been like. Some remnants of the railroad remain, and thanks to the efforts of some dedicated groups and individuals, you can even hike portions of the line. Budget the better part of a day for this trip, especially if you plan to stop and explore along the way.

Take Highway 405 north. Just past Kirkland, get onto Highway 522 eastbound. Exit onto Highway 9 northbound and take it to the City of Snohomish sign. Go right (east) on Marsh Road and follow the signs left to Airport Way. Take Airport Way past the airport (on your left) and head into Snohomish. Turn right (east) on First Street and go through the downtown area. Take a left (north) onto Union Avenue and then a right (east) onto Second Street. Go to the next stoplight (Maple Avenue). Turn left (north) and continue through the four-way stop at the corner of Maple and Pine. You are now leaving the city of Snohomish.

Bear left at the "Y" (the Flowing Lake sign). Here the road name changes to South Machias Road. You'll pass the Centennial Trailhead parking area on your right. Stay on South Machias past Dubuque Road and Centennial Middle School on your left. At the stop sign, turn right, continuing on South Machias. Pass OK Mill Road on your right. South Machias Road will turn into North Machias Road at this point. Continue until you reach Hartford Drive (28th Street NE).

At Hartford Drive (28th Street NE), turn left (north) and go about $^1/_{10}$ mile. Pull into the small parking area on the right side of the road. A brown sign identifies the former site of the City of Hartford and the starting point of the Everett and Monte Cristo Railway. This is where our tour begins.

Make a very careful U-turn and go back to the stop sign at the corner of Hartford Drive and North Machias Road. Set your trip odometer to 0.00 and turn left onto North Machias. Head east toward Granite Falls.

Odometer	Direction
0.70	Take a right and go east on Highway 92. The Everett and Monte Cristo grade ran along the right side of the present-day highway.
1.00	The old railroad grade changes over to the left side of the highway.
1.30	You'll pass Cedar Springs Bible Camp on your left. On your right, you can see (on a clear day) the majestic Cascades, including Mount Pilchuck, Whitehorse Mountain, and Three Fingers Mountain.
2.50	The old railroad grade crossed at this point to the right side of the highway. If you look carefully, you can see the railroad grade and bed in the line of trees that parallels the highway.
5.70	You are entering Granite Falls. The railroad once operated a small depot just north of Highway 92 between Anderson Avenue and Cascade Avenue. (Gas stations are scarce on the road ahead. This might be the last outpost for fuel.) Go through the town of Granite Falls.

6.50	At the second four-way stop, turn left onto the Mountain Loop Highway.

Odometer	Direction
6.80	Granite Falls High School is on your right. (Beware: The speed limit is 25 mph and is strictly enforced!)
7.00	At Gun Club Road, the old railroad bed switches back to the south side of the highway.
8.00	On your left (the north side of road) is a small parking area and a trail leading down to the Stillaguamish River. The hike is short but moderately steep. At the bottom, you can see a fish ladder that allows fish to continue their spawning trips up the river.

10.3	You'll pass Hidden Valley Road (135th Street NE) on your left.
11.0	The long hill in front of you is Sand Hill.
13.5	You are now at Tupso Pass Road (Green Mountain Road). On your right you'll find a parking area. You can park here to take a very interesting hike. Find the brick monument dedicated to the Old Robe Trail. (You can't miss it.) Almost directly behind it is a trail leading down to the historic town site of Robe. Farther down the trail, you can see examples of old railroad tunnels. Shortly after you begin your hike, you'll come to a lofty overlook that offers a spectacular view of Mount Pilchuck and the surrounding valley. If you look below to the canyon floor, you can see a millpond that was created by the (now defunct) Canyon Lumber Company. Just to the left of the millpond you will see the town site of Robe, which was built around 1892. You might also be able to see the roadbed of an old railroad wye, where trains were turned around after picking up lumber at the mill site.

Odometer   **Direction**

Continue down the trail (it's pretty well worn and easy to follow), keeping to the right until you get to the bottom, where the trail makes a sharp turn to the left. At this point, you are standing on the old railroad wye. You can almost hear the chugging of the locomotives straining to move their heavy loads. Continue down to the fork where the trail splits, and take the path to the right. About ¹/₂ mile down this path, you can see a large clearing on your right, which is the old town site of Robe. On your left is the Stillaguamish River. The river becomes a raging torrent in the spring, when the melting snow causes large amounts of water to be dumped into the canyon bottom. After the spring runoff, the river becomes docile; visitors often swim in it. However, the seemingly harmless river can still be dangerous because of the many hidden snags and submerged boulders.

Follow the trail along the riverbank, passing the old millpond on your right. (Do not remove any artifacts that you might find along the trail. Please leave them for the enjoyment of other visitors.) You'll soon come to a concrete wall that supports the trail and extends some 1,650 feet into the first railroad tunnel you'll encounter (tunnel #6). Take a look at the river as it flows past. You can see how the riverbed drops steeply, creating dangerous whitewater rapids through the gorge. You can imagine how the river could become a destructive, raging torrent. (When Charles Colby and Colgate Hoyt described this river to prospective investors, they called it a "little trout stream"!)

Proceed along the "sweeping" curve in the railbed to the tunnel entrance. The trail along this section is incomparably beautiful. As you enter the mouth (portal) of the tunnel, note that the railroad ties were set in concrete. When the tunnel was first built, the ties were set in the ground. But the railroad soon learned the first of many costly lessons. The river overflowed its banks during the spring and raged through the tunnel, carrying away support timbers and ties. Even today, at flood stage the river still courses through the tunnel. You have now traveled about 1.6 miles from the trailhead. (Not tired yet, are you?) About 300 feet down the trail after you exit tunnel #6, look to your left for a large "pool" in the river. Above the pool on the mountainside is the adit, or opening, of a prospect hole where a miner searched for valuable minerals (and found none). The hole is only a few feet deep. The Cascades are pockmarked with these reminders of the gold rush days.

Another 200 feet or so down the trail, you'll come to a nice, flat boulder that is a great place for a short break. Continue down the trail to the portal of tunnel #5. You are now 1.8 miles from the trailhead. The trail beyond this tunnel becomes very steep and quite rough. It is not suitable for young children or those who are not physically fit. We suggest that you make this the end of your hike since there is still plenty to see on the remainder of the driving tour.

If you are in good physical condition and have a burning desire to "see what's over the next hill," you can continue on, but beware of steep spots and sharp dropoffs. As you proceed, you'll see large logs in the river sitting on boulders or wedged between them. These logs were carried along the river by the strong currents and deposited there. You might also see some of the old railroad rails that were washed away in past floods.

Odometer	Direction
	About 700 feet from the exit of tunnel #5, you'll come to the open cut that was tunnel #4. It had so many problems with cave-ins and washouts that in 1911 it was dynamited and cleared. After you exit tunnel #4, the trail becomes very steep for a short distance and then heads back toward the river. (Use extreme care, and stay off the concrete culvert on the left side of the trail. This cement "path" is very dangerous. We mean it!) After another 150 feet or so, the trail again becomes steep and treacherous. If you look ahead, you can see the portal of tunnel #3. This tunnel is dangerous. Do not enter it under any circumstances! The trail beyond this point becomes indistinct and extremely steep and is loaded with dangerous pitfalls such as slippery talus slopes and sharp dropoffs. Do not go any farther— no matter what your level of experience. A brisk hike back to the trailhead from this point should take about 1 to 1½ hours. Be careful on the way back.
16.3	We're on our way again. A small general store is on your left; a gas station is ahead on the right. (These stores are not always open.)
17.1	You are now entering the Mt. Baker-Snoqualmie National Forest.

| 17.5 | The Verlot Public Service Center is on your left. On your right is a parking area. Pull in here to see an ore cart that was used during the mining days and a display section of a 700-year-old Douglas fir. |

Odometer	Direction
18.4	You are now crossing a bridge over the South Fork of the Stillaguamish River. At this point, the old railroad bed merges with the present-day highway and follows this path almost all the way to Monte Cristo.
19.6	The Hemple Creek Campground picnic area is on your left.
20.0	On your right is the site of an old prospector's camp and the Gold Basin millpond.

20.7	You are now crossing Black Creek. If you look carefully to your right, you can see two old dams at the former site of a shingle mill.
21.5	The Wiley Creek Campground is on your left. You can stop here and take a short hike on the right side of the road, up the hillside, to the site of a sinkhole. There is no trail, and the hike is obstructed by heavy vegetation and many deadfalls. The sinkhole is about 250 feet off to your right when you reach the top of the hill. It is 60 to 70 feet wide and 40 to 50 feet deep. It was created when the partially excavated railway tunnel #7 caved in, almost trapping the workers inside. There is not much else to see up here, so we suggest that you head back down to your vehicle to continue the journey, heading eastbound. The area of curves that you enter as you leave Wiley Creek Campground is where the ralroad bypassed the ill-fated tunnel #7 and was known by railroaders as "the Shoofly."

B

Roster of Equipment

Everett and Monte Cristo Railway

Compiled by Lorenz P. Schrenk

Locomotives

#1	4-6-0, 21x26-56, 6/1892, Cooke #2223. To Northern Pacific #366, Class E-7. To Cowlitz, Chehalis & Cascade #5, 2/1925.
#2	4-6-0, 21x26-56, 6/1892, Cooke #2224. To NP #367, Class E-7. Dismantled 12/1923.
#3	4-6-0, 21x26-56, 2/1893, Cooke #2225. To NP #368, Class E-7. Dismantled 12/1923.
#4	4-4-0, 18x26-63, 12/1888, Schenectady 2780. Bought secondhand. Formerly Union Pacific #618, #620, #621, #625, or #633. Renumbered Monte Cristo #99 in 1902. To NP #649, Class B-2. NP boiler #21 assigned. Dismantled 5/1919, South Tacoma.

Passenger Cars

#1	First-class coach, Barney & Smith, built 1892. Originally #A-1. To NP first-class coach #767, 5/1903. To NP second-class coach #667, 4/1909. To NP drovers car #2016, 7/1930. Retired 9/1935.
#10	First-class coach Barney & Smith, built 1892. Originally #A-10. To NP first-class coach #768, 4/1903. To NP second-class coach #668, 5/1909. To NP motor-car trailer #A-100, 9/1927. Dismantled 5/1930.
#11	First-class coach Barney & Smith, built 1892. Originally #A-11. To NP first-class coach #769, 5/1903. To NP second-class coach #669, 1/1909. Retired 12/1929.
#20	Mail and express car. Barney & Smith, built 1892. 50' length over sills, 4-wheel trucks. Originally #B-20. To NP mail and express car #116. To NP supply car S-67, 11/1923.
#21	Mail and express car. Barney & Smith, built 1892. 50' length over sills, 4-wheel trucks. Originally #B-21. To NP mail and express car #117. To NP supply car S-68, 10/1923.
#300	Coach-observation car. St. Charles Car Company, 60' length over sills, 6-wheel trucks. To NP third-class coach #662. Scrapped 2/1927.

Freight Cars

#100-102	3 cabooses. To NP cabooses, numbers unknown.
#200-220	21 boxcars. To NP 33' boxcars #11656-11671 and #11673-11675, 27'7" boxcar #11672, and 36'2" boxcar #11676.
#1-50	50 flatcars. To NP 31' flatcars #24100-24122 and #24124-24150.
?	23 flatcars. To NP 34'9" flatcar #24123 and 34' flatcars #24151-24172.
#500-534	35 gondola coal cars. To NP twelve 31' gondola cars #59965-59976 and twenty-three 34' gondola cars #59977-59999.

Maintenance-of-Way Equipment

#1	Leslie rotary snowplow. To NP rotary plow #8.
?	Portable pile driver. To NP pile driver, number unknown.
?	Barnhardt steam shovel. To NP steam shovel #2.

Miscellaneous Notes
- There might have been a Baldwin-built 0-4-0 on the E&MC when the road first opened.
- The E&MC boxcars might have been built by the Peninsular Car Company.
- One E&MC boxcar was purchased from the Chicago, Burlington & Quincy.
- All E&MC equipment was transferred to the Monte Cristo Railway in August 1900.
- Forty-eight of the MC flatcars were equipped with wood racks.
- All E&MC/MC equipment was transferred to NP and renumbered in 1903.

Hartford Eastern Railway

Compiled by Phil Woodhouse

Gas Cars

No number	White (manufacturer) open four-wheel bus, 1915. Powered by a 4-cylinder, 40-HP engine. 10 to 15 seats.
#1	White 1.5-ton truck chassis with a wooden bus body built by New Haven Carriage. Cost: $2,834 in 1916.
#2	Signal 2.5-ton truck chassis with a wooden bus body built by New Haven Carriage. Cost: $3,296 in 1917.
#3	Hofius Steel and Equipment gas car, 1915. 125-HP, 6-cylinder engine with a steel body. It could carry two tons of freight along with 30 passengers. It sported two 33-inch rear driver wheels and four 28-inch truck-mounted pony wheels. Cost: $8,000. Sold to Valley & Siletz Railroad of Hoskins, Oregon, in 1918 for $5,000. Rebuilt in 1923 at a cost of $3,168. Scrapped in 1945.
#3*	Studebaker, 1915, with a wooden body. Cost: $1,832.
#21	White truck chassis, probably the rebuilt #1 gas car, with a metal bus body built by the New Haven Carriage Company. It had two rear driver wheels and four front pony wheels mounted on a truck. This was the first of three gas cars that were the workhorses of the line from about 1917 to the early 1930s. It was distinguished by the rear of the roof being flush with the body (no overhang). The front of the roof did overhang the windshield area. Oval opera windows were located just ahead of the rear of the coach, and the rear window was rectangular. The driver, in the original version, was exposed to the elements.
#22	Signal truck chassis, probably the rebuilt #2 gas car, with a metal bus body built by the New Haven Carriage Company. It had two rear driver wheels and four truck-mounted front pony wheels. Both the rear and front of the roof overhung the body. The car had no opera windows, and the rear window was rectangular with a vertical strut in the center. The front fenders sloped forward, away from the body. The metal body was sculpted inward along the sides of the car, and the rear driver wheels were partially hidden by skirts that were flush with the body panels.
#23	White truck chassis fitted with a metal bus body, 1917 or earlier. The car had two rear driver wheels and four truck-mounted front pony wheels. It had oval opera windows just ahead of the rear of the car and an oval rear window. The roof overhung both the rear and the front of the car. The car had roll-down isinglass windows along both sides. The body was flat-sided, with three storage compartments along the lower left side and two along the lower right side. (The place for the third was taken up by the door.) The front fenders were rounded to contour with the pony wheels.
#24	Stevens-Duryea touring car built in 1911 and bought used for $529. Converted to rail service between 1917 and 1926. It had only four wheels.
#25	The Black Mariah. Named for a notorious New York paddy wagon, this was Wyatt Rucker's personal car. Except for the earlier Hofius car (when delivered), it was the only piece of the Rucker's equipment that was not painted white. It was a Mitchell car fitted with gun carriage wheels in the rear and a four-wheel railway truck in the front.

* It is not known why there were two #3 gas cars.

#100   Built by Brill, model 55, c/n 22785, in 1929. It had 43 seats, a 68-HP Brill engine, and a riveted all-steel body. Cost: $17,471.68. It was built to look similar to the popular interurban cars that were plying the rails between major cities. But the car was so heavy and underpowered that it could barely get up the grades of the Hartford Eastern, much less carry the freight and passengers for which it was designed. Nonetheless, it served the line until the Hartford Eastern's demise a few years later, when it was sold for $4,000 to the Skagit River Railway in April 1936 as their second #4. It was sold in June 1954 to the Dulien Steel Company, the company that scrapped the SRR, for $377. It was sold in 1956 or 1957 to Morrison-Knudson on the Northern Pacific Eagle Gorge line change and was cut down to a "pickup truck" look. The car was last seen in 1962 in a scrapyard in the Ballard neighborhood of Seattle.

The Northern Pacific's #309 at Lowell in 1892. The 3S Railway leased it from the Northern Pacific for use as its construction locomotive. *(Everett Public Library Collection #096, King & Baskerville photo)*

A Porter locomotive at work for Bryant Lumber & Shingle Company in Bryant. This locomotive was likely the Northern Pacific's "Otter Tail," one of its original locomotives that was later used to build the Everett and Monte Cristo line between Everett and the smelter before being sold to the logging company. *(John Labbe Collection, Darius Kinsey photo)*

The Everett and Monte Cristo's #1 locomotive in Granite Falls in 1906, after it became the Northern Pacific's #366. The Chehalis, Cowlitz & Cascade Railroad bought it in 1925 as its #5. *(John Ammann Collection, Courtesy of Everett Hobbycraft)*

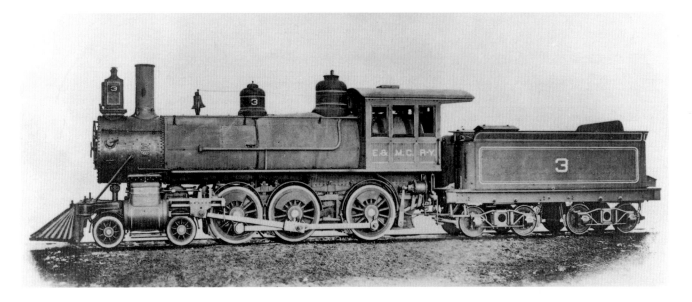

A Cooke Locomotive Works builder's photograph of the Everett and Monte Cristo's #3 locomotive, which was built in 1893. This locomotive later became the Northern Pacific's #368, Class E-7. *(Railroad Museum of Pennsylvania, negative #0422123)*

The Northern Pacific's #367, Class E-7, at Pasco in 1916. This locomotive was built for the Everett and Monte Cristo Railway as its #2. The tender shown here is not the original tender, and the bell and sand dome have been switched. The Northern Pacific also added a second sand dome between the bell and the steam dome. When new, this locomotive was identical to the Everett and Monte Cristo's #3, shown in the previous photograph. *(Dan Cozine Collection, Criles photo)*

The Union Pacific Railroad's locomotive #632. The Everett and Monte Cristo bought a locomotive similar to this from the Union Pacific for use as its #4 (and later #99). This locomotive became the Northern Pacific's #649, Class B-2. *(Oregon Historical Society #UP632, Roberts Collection)*

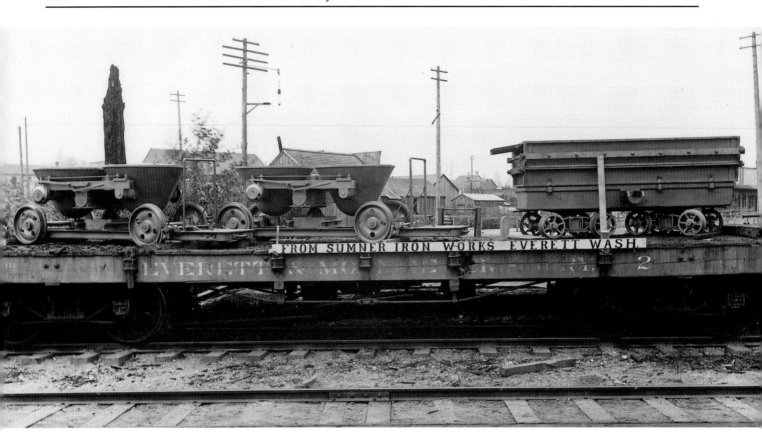

A Sumner Iron Works builder's photograph showing cars that were probably destined for a smelter. This photo, taken at the Sumner yard in Everett, shows the Everett and Monte Cristo's 31-foot flatcar #2, which later became the Northern Pacific's #24101. *(Courtesy of Tom Speranzo)*

No. 8.   **ROTARY SNOWPLOW**

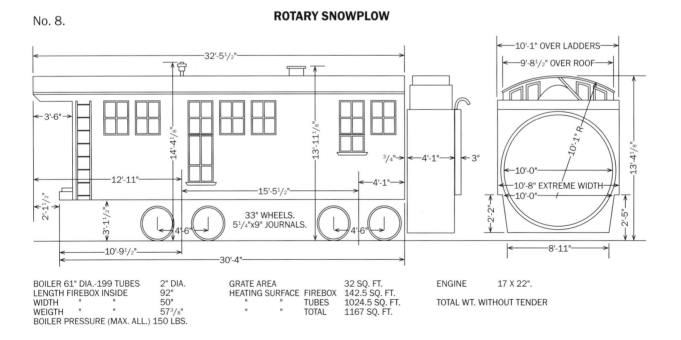

BOILER 61" DIA.-199 TUBES   2" DIA.   GRATE AREA   32 SQ. FT.   ENGINE   17 X 22".
LENGTH FIREBOX INSIDE   92"   HEATING SURFACE FIREBOX   142.5 SQ. FT.
WIDTH   "   "   50"   "   "   TUBES   1024.5 SQ. FT.   TOTAL WT. WITHOUT TENDER
WEIGTH   "   "   57³/₈"   "   "   TOTAL   1167 SQ. FT.
BOILER PRESSURE (MAX. ALL.) 150 LBS.

A dimensioned drawing of the Everett and Monte Cristo's Leslie rotary snowplow. *(Drawing by James D. Kramer)*

SECOND CLASS SMOKER
NO. 5668 & 669

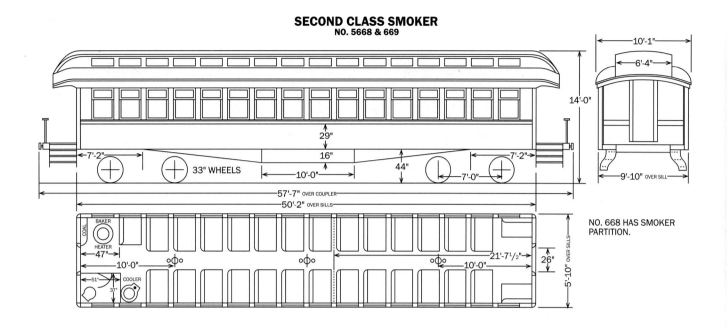

NO. 668 HAS SMOKER
PARTITION.

SECOND CLASS COACH
NO. 662

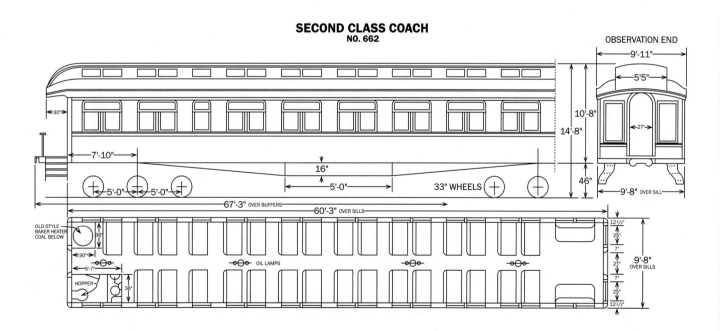

Dimensioned drawings of two of the Everett and Monte Cristo's passenger cars. *(Drawing by James D. Kramer)*

Gas car #22 and the little rotary snowplow at Silverton after many years of hard use.

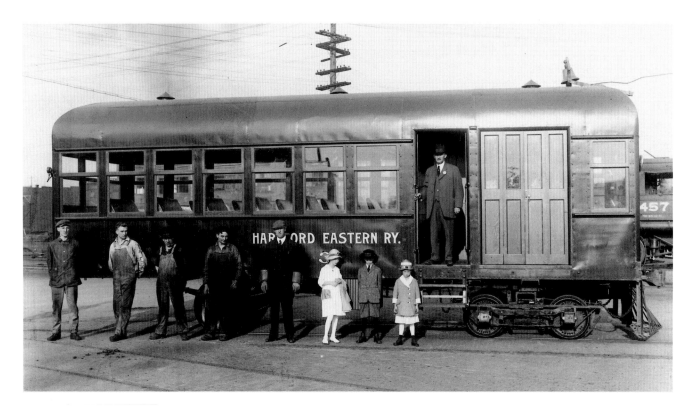

Gas car #3 of the Hartford Eastern at the Hofius yard in Seattle in 1915. The car had just been finished and was ready for delivery to the Ruckers, who probably painted the car white. The #3 sported a 6-cylinder, 125-horsepower engine, and 30 passenger seats and could haul 2 tons of freight. *(Museum of History and Industry, Pemco Webster & Stevens Collection)*

Gas car #21 of the Hartford Eastern at the approach to Red Bridge just below Silverton. The car is towing the utility trailer that was used to haul goods, materials, and (on nice days) passengers up the line and garbage back down the line. *(Enid Nordlund Collection)*

(following page) Another view of gas car #21 on Red Bridge. The logs in the foreground are the kind of material that was hurtled down the Stillaguamish River during the rainy season. *(Enid Nordlund Collection)*

Gas car #22 of the Hartford Eastern just after being turned on the Monte Cristo turntable. *(Phil Woodhouse Collection, John A. Juleen photo)*

Gas car #22 at the Inn at Big Four. In tow is the larger passenger trailer. The car points east toward Monte Cristo. *(University of Washington, Special Collections Division, negative #UW4060)*

Gas car #22 at the Hartford Eastern's gas car barn in Hartford. It is sitting on a small turntable used to turn the gas cars around. *(Bob Thorsen Collection)*

Gas car #23 of the Hartford Eastern at Hartford Junction, towing a trailer. Note the distinctive rear oval window. *(Enid Nordlund Collection)*

Gas car #23 at Hartford Junction. Note the roll-up canvas sides that enabled passengers to enjoy the open air on pleasant days. *(Enid Nordlund Collection)*

Gas car #100 of the Hartford Eastern, which was built to resemble an interurban car. The woefully underpowered car is shown here at the Inn at Big Four, facing west. *(Phil Woodhouse Collection)*

The Black Mariah, Wyatt Rucker's personal car. It was a Mitchell motor car with military gun carriage wheels that enabled it to run on the rails. *(Bob Thorsen Collection)*

C

Bridges and Other Landmarks

Bridges

Compiled by Phil Woodhouse

Note: This information is from the original engineering drawings. Over time, some bridges were changed or filled in, and in some cases the track itself was redirected, rendering the original distances obsolete.

No.	Type	Length	Height*	Distance**	Notes
1	Pile	147'	15'	4,166'	
2	Pile	95.1'	9.6'	5,444'	
3	Pile	134.1'	7.5'	7,312'	
4	Unknown	~500'	36'	31,176'	1
5	Timber trestle	91'	17.5'	42,981'	
6	Timber trestle	126'	40'	43,111'	
7	Frame trestle	75.5'	22'	43,374'	
8	Frame trestle	269.5'	47.5'	45,009'	
9	Unknown	250'	55'	45,698'	2
10	Frame trestle	180'	25'	46,139'	
11	Unknown	280'	48'	49,110'	3
12	Unknown	262'	53'	49,601'	
N/A	Howe truss deck span	~150' single span	~70'	49,700	4
13	Pile	94.5'	12.5'	49,863'	
14	Howe truss deck span	150' single span	74'	53,987'	
15	Unknown	68'	12.5'	65.601'	5

No.	Type	Length	Height*	Distance**	Notes
16	Unknown	~60'	12.5'	65,519'	6
17	Pile	121.2'	12.5'	76,952'	
18	Howe truss throughspan	126' single span	25'	80,746'	7
18.1	Pile	368'	10'	81,308'	8
18.2	Unknown	80'	5'	81,766'	
19	Pile	111'	4'	84,245'	
20	Frame trestle	85.2'	25'	88,289'	
21	Frame trestle	191'	24'	92,611'	
22	Frame trestle	46'	5'	96,559'	
23	Unknown	20'	12'	97,794'	
24	Frame trestle	43'	5'	102,658'	
25	Frame trestle	46.2'	12.5'	104,786'	
26	Frame trestle	45'	12'	105,588'	
27	Timber trestle	137'	15'	109,010'	
28	Frame trestle	91.1'	12'	110,541'	
29	Frame trestle	104'	17.5'	112,209'	
30	Unknown	175'	10'	116,330'	9
31	Frame trestle	104'	13'	118,502'	
32	Pony span	60'	15'	124,345'	
	Pile	46' approach to H. T.	3'	131,100'	
33	Howe truss throughspan	126.3' single span	24'	131,146'	10
	Pile	127' approach to H. T.	15'	131,273'	
34	Pile	63'	12.6'	133,920'	
35	Unknown	150'	15'	134,220'	Filled before 1907
36	Pile	637'	22.5'	136,439'	The Sinkhole
37	Frame trestle	88'	12'	144,186'	
37A	Frame trestle	89.3'	6'	144,451'	11
38	Unknown	16'	6'	148,876'	
38.1	Unknown	15'	7'	149,141'	8
39	Pile	232.4'	6'	155,142'	
40	Pile	111.3'	12'	158,324'	
41	Pile	507.9'	8'	160,650'	
42	Pile	204.7'	8'	161,632'	
43	Pile	186'	12'	166,327'	
44	Pile	59.3'	6'	167,237'	
45	Pile	60'	5'	168,422'	
46	Pile	59.6'	5'	170,385'	
47	Pile	60'	8'	171,158'	
48	Pile	90'	6'	173,093'	
49	Frame trestle	45'	6'	180,193'	
50	Frame trestle	75.4'	12'	181,495'	
51	Frame trestle	119.3'	26'	184,573'	

No.	Type	Length	Height*	Distance**	Notes
52	Frame trestle	177.6'	21.2'	187,955'	
53	Unknown	15'	5'	188,406'	
54	Frame trestle	59.5'	8'	189,688'	
	snowshed	180'	n/a	199,372'	
55	Frame trestle	195.4'	25'	199,372'	
56	Pile	317'	10'	202,596'	12
57	Pile	120.1'	12'	212,408'	
58	Unknown	60'	5'	215,630'	
59	Frame trestle	80'	Unknown	217,114'	
60	Frame trestle	105.1'	Unknown	218,190'	
61	Frame trestle	300'	Unknown	221,608'	13
62	Frame trestle	209'	Unknown	Unknown	14
63	Frame trestle	789.9'	Unknown	Unknown	15
64	Frame trestle	359'	Unknown	Unknown	16

* Maximum height above the ground or water surface crossed by this structure.

** Distance from the main head block at Hartford. Measured to the down-track end of the structure.

1 Not on the drawing. Probably bridged a 36-foot deep gully but was later filled.

2 Not on the drawing. Probably bridged a 55-foot deep gully but was later filled.

3 Not on the drawing. Probably bridged a 48-foot deep gully but was later filled.

4 Immediately adjacent to the Monte Cristo right-of-way on the Johnson-Dean Lumber Company's tracks where they switched off at the station stop of Cutoff.

5 Carried away by a slide in 1907.

6 Filled in May 1910.

7 Originally a double-span consisting of two Howe truss throughspans placed end to end. Following the disastrous floods of 1897, the river was channelized and the bridge was replaced with the single throughspan Howe Truss listed here. Notice the long pile bridge approaches to this span. Bridge #18 had a 25-foot-high, 215-foot-long pile-type western approach starting at 80,528 feet and a 12-foot-high, 345.2-foot-long pile-type eastern approach at 80.869 feet.

8 Added later. The engineers used the decimal numbering scheme so that they didn't have to renumber the existing subsequent bridges.

9 Filled.

10 Commonly known as the "Red Bridge." The area is still known as Red Bridge, with Red Bridge Forest Service Campground located in the vicinity. The highway bridge that crosses the Stillaguamish River is even painted red (as of February 1998).

11 Originally bridge #37. The engineers renamed it 37A when they built a new bridge at 144,486 feet because they didn't want to renumber the subsequent bridges.

12 Located at the same crossing of the South Fork of the Sauk River as the current Twin Bridges, which carry the Monte Cristo access road.

13 The trestle that ushered the main line into Monte Cristo across the South Fork of the Sauk River.

14 The trestle that carried the concentrator spur from the Monte Cristo yards toward the switchback on its way up the valley.

15 The trestle that carried the concentrator spur across Glacier Creek to the concentrator mill and the end of the line.

16 The trestle that carried the concentrator spur back to the offices and assay buildings near Monte Cristo.

Milepost Listing of Bridges and Other Landmarks

Compiled by Lorenz P. Schrenk

Note: This information is from Northern Pacific Railroad records (1917). Mileposts are to the east end of bridges and tunnels and to the headblock of switches.

Milepost	Bridge #	Description or Lengths/spans	Built or Rebuilt	Notes
Hartford				
0.8	1	147/10	1914	Trestle; 11 bents; Pilchuck Creek Rucker Bros. Spur, 502'
1.02	2	95/6	1914	7 bents; Pilchuck Creek
1.39	3	134/9	1914	13 bents; Pilchuck Creek
2.59				Lochloy: freight house 20x16: spur
2.73				Woodland Farms Spur Sullivan Brothers Spur 341' Sulbro?
5				Parker Spur?
5.9	4	Not listed, was 300"		Filled by 1915
5.92				Small stream; no bridge
6.2				Granite Falls Spur
6.29				Granite Falls; depot 71x24
6.34				Chappel, Ewald & Swarz Spur
6.7				Wye: with tail to Sobey Mfg. Co. Logging railroad
7.58				Small lake by track; Way side?
8.14	5	91/6	1914	Trestle; 7 bents; by Stillaguamish River
8.16	6	120/8	1914	Trestle; 9 bents; by Stillaguamish River
8.2	7	75/5	1914	Trestle; 6 bents; by Stillaguamish River
8.52	8	264/18	1913	Trestle; 19 bents; over stream for Hubbard Lake
8.65	9	Not listed, was 241'	1914	Filled by 1915 Temporary flume for loco water
8.74	10	183/12	1914	Trestle; 13 bents Siding; crosses bridge 10^1/$_2$
9.33	10^1/$_2$	7 bents		
	11			Deep ravine; filled by 1915
9.42		68/5	1912	Siding
	None	91/6	1915	
	12	Not listed; was 150'		Ravine; filled by 1915
	12^1/$_2$	175/?		Out of use/abandoned
		106/7		Johnson Dean connection Cutoff; depot

Milepost	Bridge #	Description or Lengths/spans	Built or Rebuilt	Notes
9.57	12$\frac{1}{3}$	1200/80	1910	Spur; crosses river
	13	Not listed; was 105'		Filled by 1915
9.98	13$\frac{1}{3}$	94/6	1915	7 bents
10.22	14	Howe truss deck; 150'	1914	Trestle approach; 8 bents; Stillaguamish 1st Xing
				Tunnel #1
				Deep cut
				Tunnel #2
				Siding
				Overhead crossing
				Powder house
12.4	15	68/5	1913	Trestle; 6 bents
	16	Not listed; was 60'		Filled by 1915
				Tunnel #3
				Cut (tunnel #4 daylighted)
				Tunnel #5
				Tunnel #5
				Siding
				Robe
				Wye; Canyon Head?
14.6	17	121/8	1907	Pile bridge and trestle; 9 bents; over stream
				Cranberry Creek
				Spur, 480"
				Stead spur; 297'
15.25	18	Howe truss thru; 126'	1910	Pile approaches; 40 bents; Stillaguamish 2nd Xing
15.4	18	368/25	1915	26 bents
15.49	18.1	79/5	1911	6 bents
15.96	19	110/7	1910	8 bents; over stream; Hawthorne Creek
16.7	20	85/6	1910	Trestle; 7 bents; over stream
				Triple Creek
				Spur; 749'; Turlo
17.55	21	190/13	1910	Trestle; 14 bents; over stream; Heather Creek
				Verlot; siding, 366'
18.29	22	46/3	1911	Trestle; 4 bents
18.52	23	20/1	1911	Trestle; 2 bents
				Section house; toolhouse
				Bogardus
19.44	24	44/3	1910	Trestle; 4 bents; over stream; 22 Creek
				Gold Basin
19.83	25	46/3	1910	Trestle; 4 bents; over stream
20	26	45/3	1907	Trestle; 4 bents
				Hemple spur 511'
20.64	27	134/9	1907	Trestle; 10 bents; edge of river
				Mackie Mill Co.; spur 353'

Milepost	Bridge #	Description or Lengths/spans	Built or Rebuilt	Notes
20.94	28	96/6	1907	Trestle; 7 bents; over stream
21.25	29	104/7	1907	Trestle; 8 bents; over stream; Wisconsin Creek
21.6	30	Not listed; was 150'		Filled by 1915 Tunnel #7; abandoned; 18 and 24 degree curves
22.46	31	104.7	1910	Trestle; 8 bents; over stream; Schweizer Creek Tyree
23.55	32	Howe truss pony; 60'	1914	Trestle approach; 15 bents; over stream Boardman Creek
24.83	33	Howe truss thru; 126'	1914	Trestle approach; Stillaguamish 3rd Xing Sunnyside?
25.36	34	62/4	1910	5 bents; over stream
	35	Not listed; was 135'		Filled by 1915
25.84	36	619/52	1911	43 bents; by river; on a slide; out of alignment Waldheim
27.31	37	90/6	1907	Trestle; 7 bents; over stream; Marten Creek
28.2	38	17/1	1910	Trestle; 2 bents; over stream 45 Mine spur Silverton siding
29			1896	Silverton depot
29.38	39	231/16	1914	17 bents; over stream
29.99	40	111/7	1910	8 bents; over stream Bonanza Queen; spur 252'
30.52	41	416/32	1914	36 bents
30.61	42	204/13	1910	14 bents; over stream
31.54	43	186/11	1907	12 bents; over stream
31.67	44	60/4	1907	5 bents; over stream
31.9	45	60/4	1910	5 bents; filled by 1922 Inn at Big Four
32.27	46	60/4	1907	Trestle; 5 bents; platform 8x20
32.49	47	60/4	1910	5 bents
32.78	48	90/6	1907	Trestle; 7 bents; over stream
34.13	49	45/3	1907	Trestle; 4 bents; over stream
34.37	50	75/5	1910?	Trestle; 6 bents; over stream
34.96	51	120/8	1907	Trestle; 9 bents; over stream
35.6	52	176/12	1907	Trestle; 13 bents; near Palmer Creek
35.68	53	15/1	1907	Trestle; 2 bents; filled by 1922
35.93	54	60/4	1907	Trestle; 5 bents; beside Palmer Creek Palmer Lake Barlow Pass

Milepost	Bridge #	Description or Lengths/spans	Built or Rebuilt	Notes
37.76			1902	Snowshed
37.86	55	194/13	1907	Trestle; 14 bents
38.37	56	317/18	1910	19 bents; Sauk River Weden Creek spur 228' Weden Creek
40.23	57	120/8	1907	9 bents
	58	80/4	1903	Trestle; switchback below town
	59	60/3	1903	Trestle; 4 bents; switchback below town
41.13	60	105/7	1909	Trestle, 8 bents; switchback below town
41.33	61	300/21	1909	Trestle; 21 bents; Sauk River
41.98				Monte Cristo depot
	62	270'		Trestle; yard and concentrator switchback
	63	780'		On concentrator spur/ switchback
	64	300'		On concentrator spur/ switchback

D A Monte Cristo Gallery

Looking down the hogback at Monte Cristo sometime between 1895 and 1897. The Everett and Monte Cristo Railway main line enters the town from right of center. The switchback to the United Concentration Company's concentrator is to the right. A locomotive switches cars in the photo's center. On the opposite side of the tracks is the government town of Monte Cristo, which operated under a federal charter, while in the foreground is the town site of Monte Cristo, which operated under a charter from the state of Ohio. The building with the large T-shaped roof, just to the right of center, is the railroad station. This began as the only sawmill in town and was converted to a station depot when the railway was completed and lumber could be cheaply shipped into town. *(Everett Public Library Collection, G. W. Kirk Photo)*

A small portion of a photo of Monte Cristo taken in 1894. The original negative is 18 inches high by 36 inches wide. The main line of the Everett and Monte Cristo Railway enters from below and curves toward the yards. The concentrator spur line crosses the trestle toward the left. On the left is Dumas Street, the commercial center of the town. The nearest building on the left, the Rialto Hotel, burned to the ground in 1895. It was fortunate that the entire town did not go up in smoke with it. The nearest building to the right of Dumas Street is the Pioneer Market. To the right, locomotive #3 hides behind a crummy, waiting to haul the daily passenger train back to Everett. The South Fork of the Sauk River flows beneath the trestle bridges. *(Frank LaRoche photo)*

Looking out one of the guest windows of the Royal Hotel in Monte Cristo. Note the two-story outhouses, complete with catwalks from their attached buildings, built to accommodate the needs of residents during the long winter months. The steep pitch of the roofs were necessary because the snow could accumulate to depths of 15 feet. *(Enid Nordlund Collection)*

(following page) Looking down the hogback at Monte Cristo sometime between 1895 and 1897. The Everett and Monte Cristo Railway main line enters the town from right of center. The switchback to the United Concentration Company's concentrator is to the right. A locomotive switches cars in the photo's center. On the opposite side of the tracks is the government town of Monte Cristo, which operated under a federal charter, while in the foreground is the town site of Monte Cristo, which operated under a charter from the state of Ohio. The building with the large T-shaped roof, just to the right of center, is the railroad station. This began as the only sawmill in town and was converted to a station depot when the railway was completed and lumber could be cheaply shipped into town. *(Everett Public Library Collection)*

Town of Monte Cristo from the Cascade of Sunday Creek.

The town of Monte Cristo taken from just below Mercedes Street near the confluence of Sunday Creek and '76 Creek. This photo clearly shows the log cribbing that supported much of Dumas street, the main thoroughfare of the town. This photo was taken just about 1900 as witnessed by the new Royal Hotel, formerly the Rockefeller House, seen at the far right of the line of buildings. *(Everett Public Library Collection, Gerwys Michal donation)*

Monte Cristo as seen from Mercedes Street in the early 1900s. The second building on the right is the Royal Hotel, formerly named the Rockefeller House until Rockefeller withdrew his financial support from the town. The main line of the railroad can been seen entering the town just above the white building left of center. The buildings of the Government Town and the Anaconda Mining Claim are seen in the distance to the left. This portion of Mercedes street, as well as most of Dumas street, are supported by log cribbing. *(Everett Public Library Collection, Gerwys Michal donation)*

On a hazy summer day, Wilmans Peak looms above Monte Cristo. Taken from the Hartford Eastern rail yard, this photo shows the Royal Hotel (later the Casscrest Inn, the Monte Cristo Inn, and formerly the Rockefeller House) high on Dumas Street, gleaming in its coat of white paint. *(Enid Nordlund Collection)*

Wilmans Peak graces the skyline in this view of Monte Cristo in the early 1920s. In the immediate foreground is the railroad turntable, and to the right and center is the Boston-American Mining Company's concentrator. *(Enid Nordlund Collection)*

E

Selected Depot Maps and Drawings

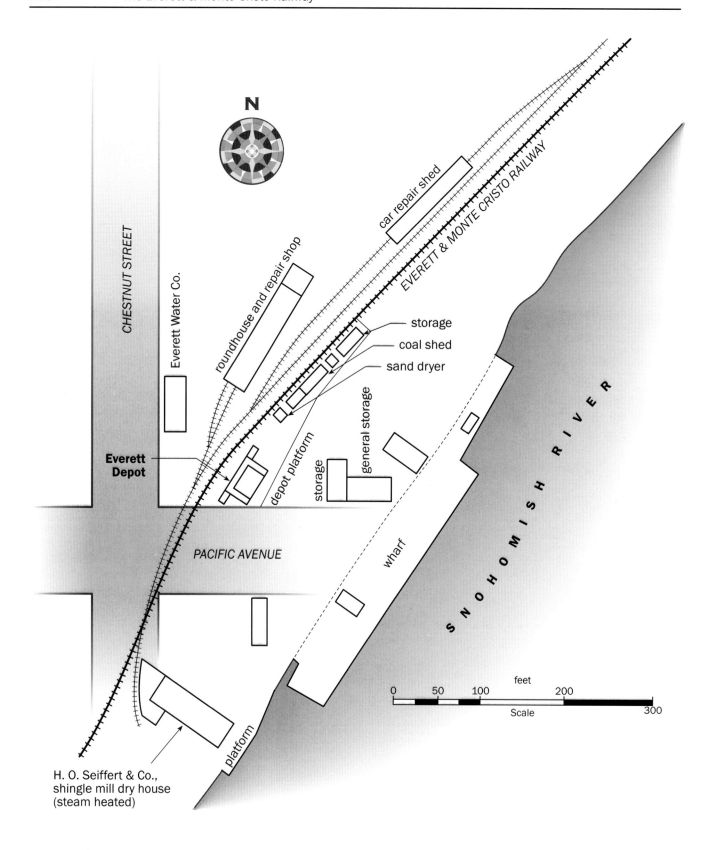

N

CHESTNUT STREET

Everett Water Co.

roundhouse and repair shop

car repair shed

EVERETT & MONTE CRISTO RAILWAY

storage
coal shed
sand dryer

general storage

Everett Depot

depot platform

storage

wharf

PACIFIC AVENUE

SNOHOMISH RIVER

platform

H. O. Seiffert & Co., shingle mill dry house (steam heated)

feet
0   50   100   200
Scale   300

Everett Depot Area

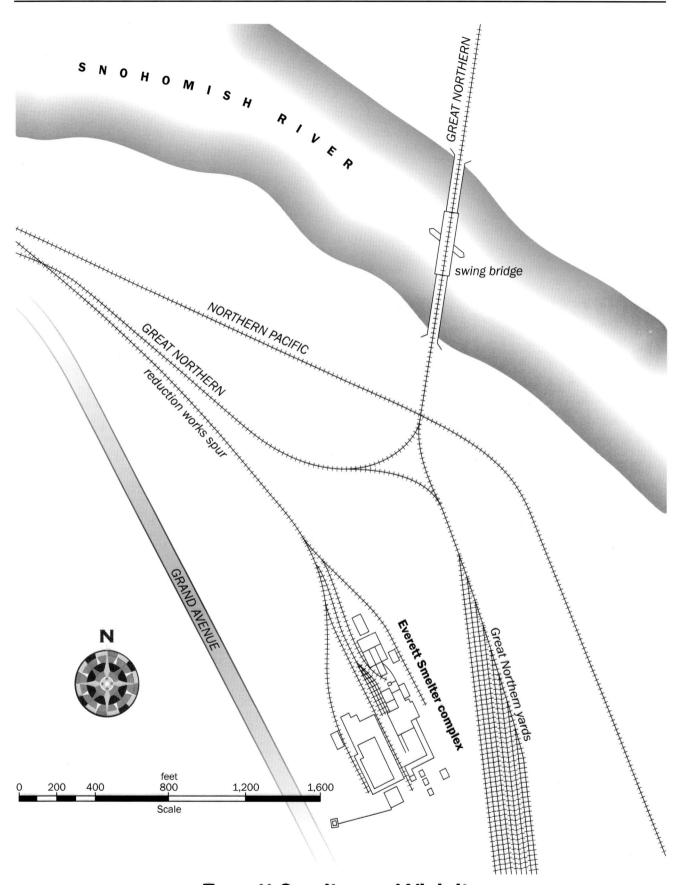

Everett Smelter and Vicinity

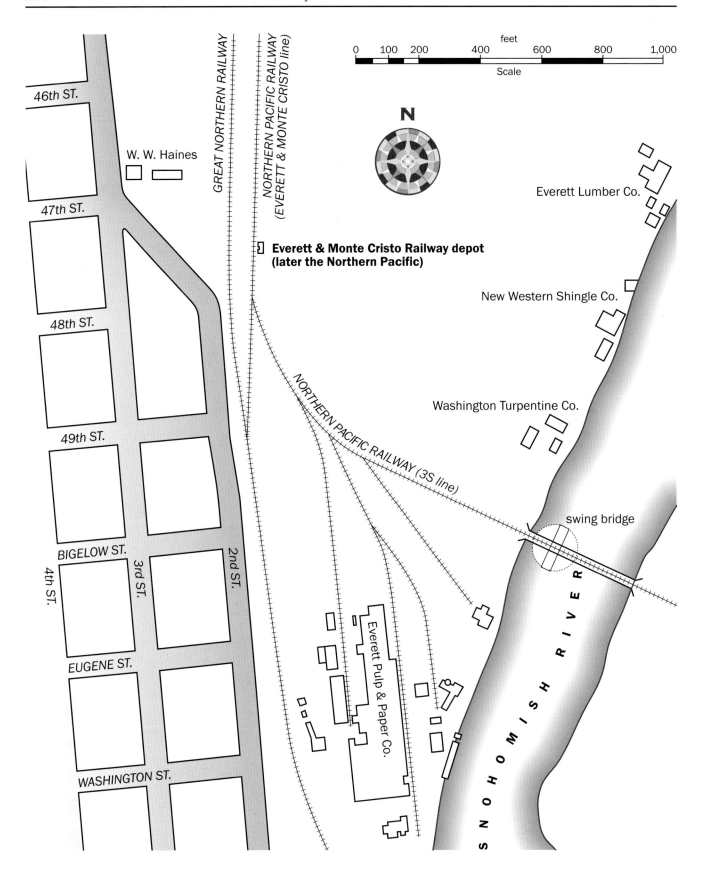

46th ST.

W. W. Haines

47th ST.

48th ST.

49th ST.

BIGELOW ST.

4th ST.

3rd ST.

2nd ST.

EUGENE ST.

WASHINGTON ST.

GREAT NORTHERN RAILWAY

NORTHERN PACIFIC RAILWAY
(EVERETT & MONTE CRISTO line)

**Everett & Monte Cristo Railway depot
(later the Northern Pacific)**

NORTHERN PACIFIC RAILWAY (3S line)

Everett Pulp & Paper Co.

feet

0   100 200   400   600   800   1,000

Scale

N

Everett Lumber Co.

New Western Shingle Co.

Washington Turpentine Co.

swing bridge

SNOHOMISH RIVER

Lowell Depot Area

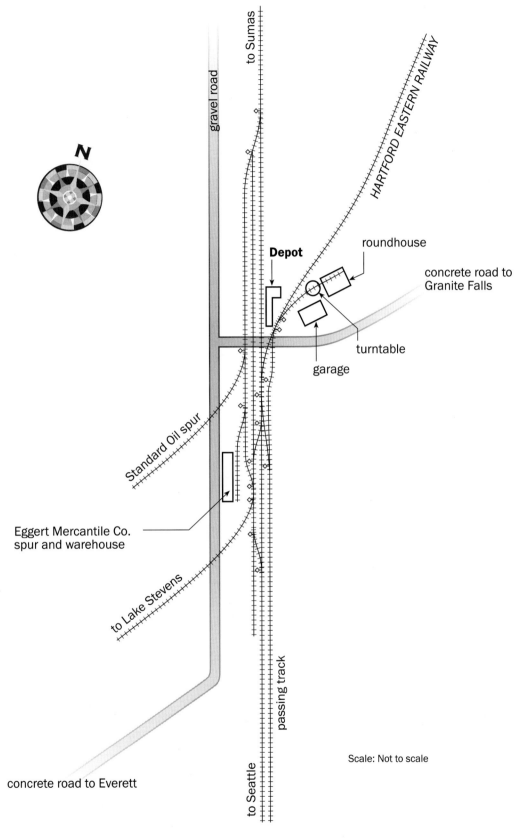

**Hartford Eastern Railway Connection
to the Northern Pacific Railway**

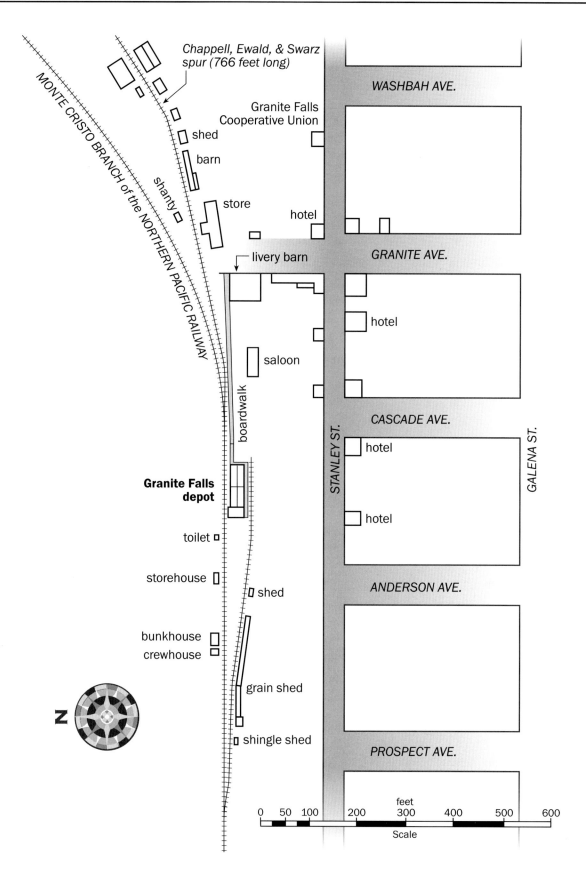

Granite Falls

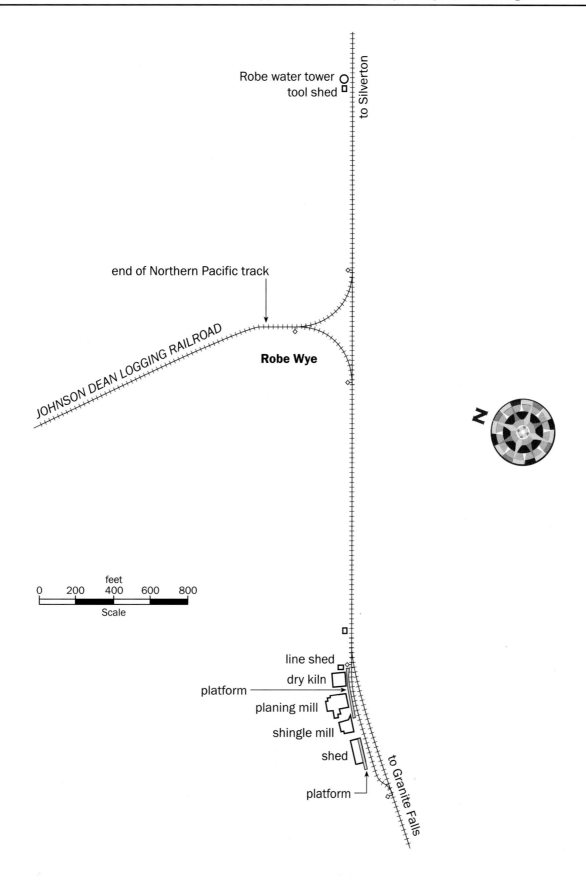

Robe water tower

tool shed

to Silverton

end of Northern Pacific track

JOHNSON DEAN LOGGING RAILROAD

Robe Wye

N

feet
0   200   400   600   800
Scale

line shed

dry kiln

platform

planing mill

shingle mill

shed

platform

to Granite Falls

Robe Wye and Vicinity

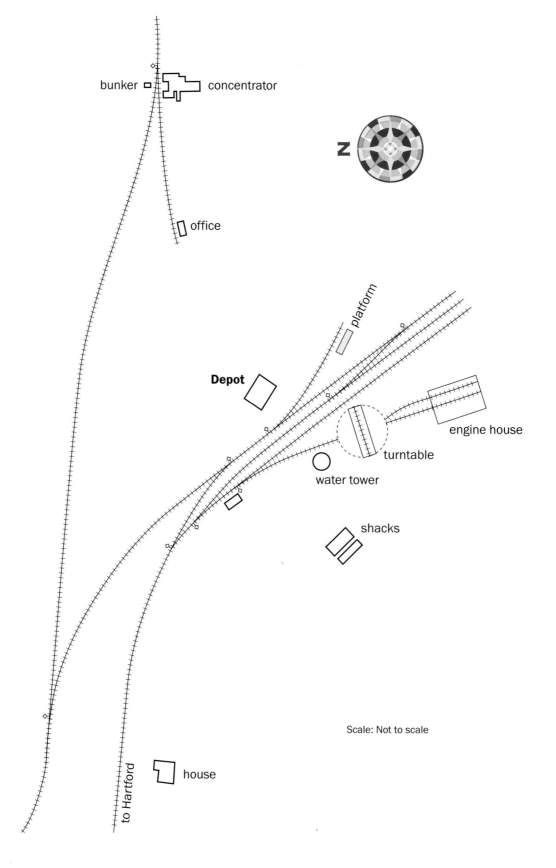

bunker

concentrator

office

N

platform

Depot

engine house

turntable

water tower

shacks

Scale: Not to scale

to Hartford

house

Monte Cristo circa 1904

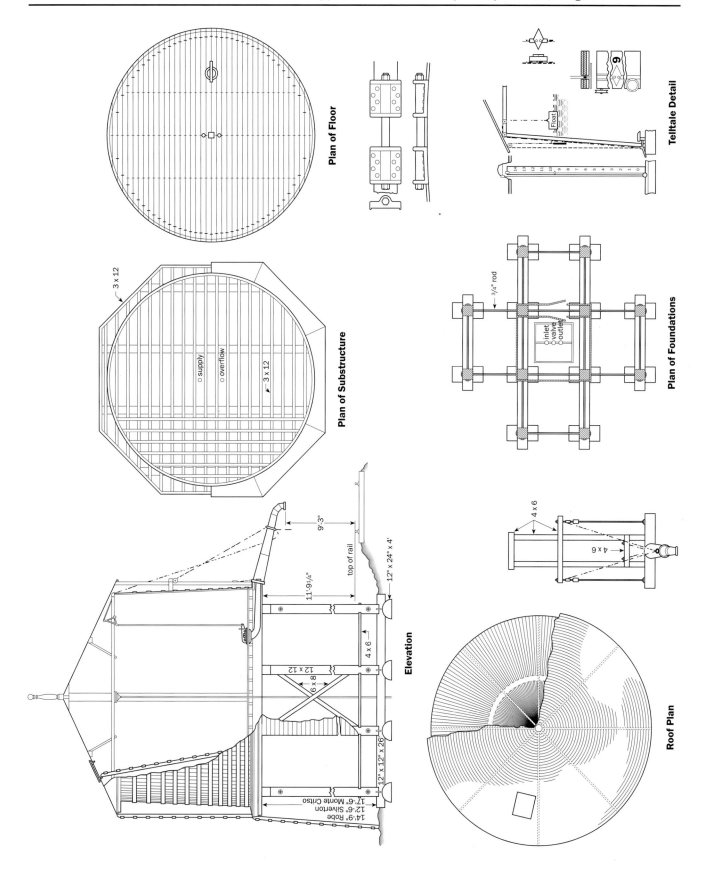

Water Tower

(Drawing courtesy Phil Schnell with James D. Kramer)

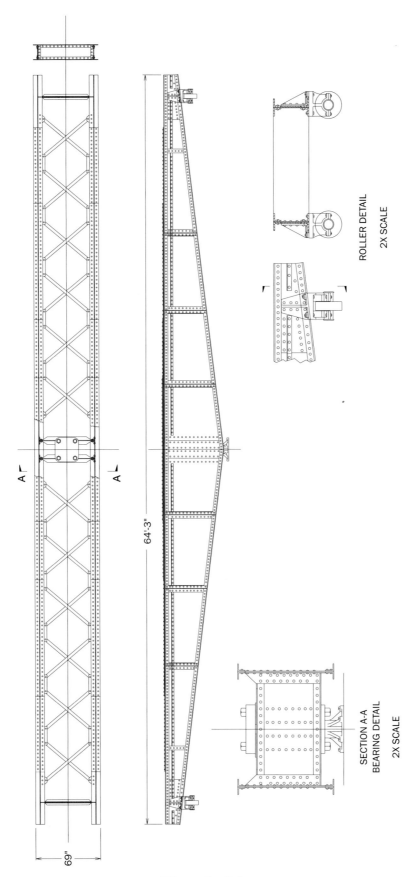

ROLLER DETAIL
2X SCALE

SECTION A-A
BEARING DETAIL
2X SCALE

64'-3"

69"

A

A

Turntable

(Built by Union Bridge Company, Athens, Pennsylvania
Drawing by Phil Schnell)

Index

Italic page numbers refer to photos, illustrations, or information in photo captions.

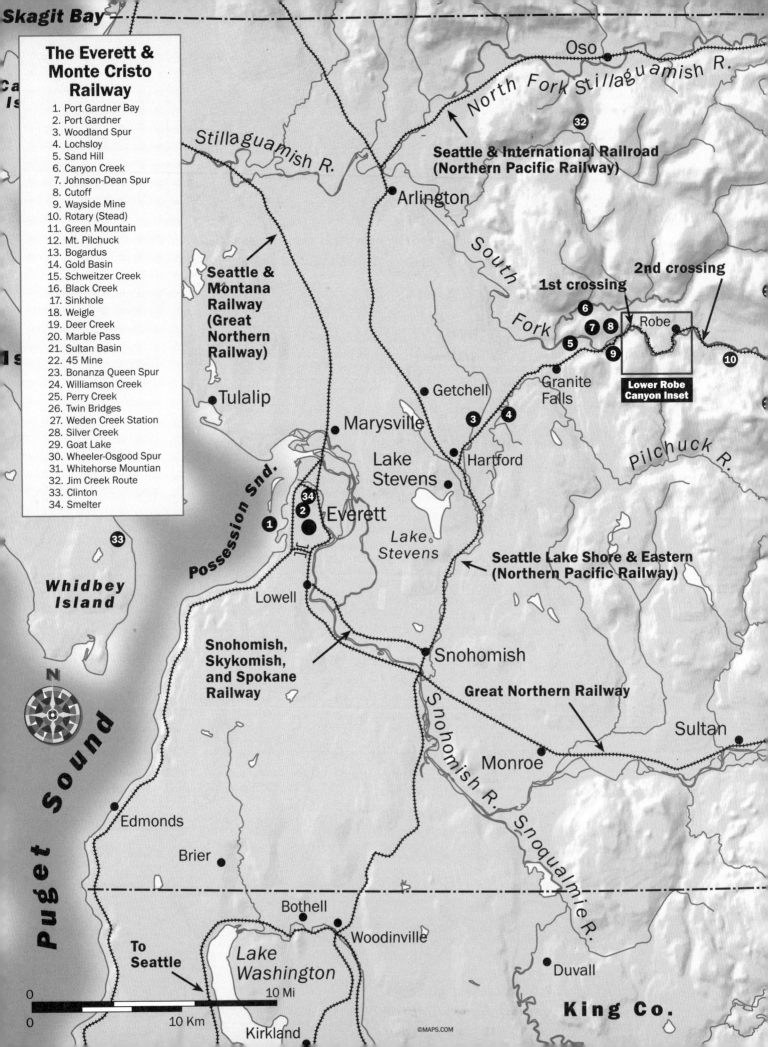

Skagit Bay

The Everett & Monte Cristo Railway

1. Port Gardner Bay
2. Port Gardner
3. Woodland Spur
4. Lochsloy
5. Sand Hill
6. Canyon Creek
7. Johnson-Dean Spur
8. Cutoff
9. Wayside Mine
10. Rotary (Stead)
11. Green Mountain
12. Mt. Pilchuck
13. Bogardus
14. Gold Basin
15. Schweitzer Creek
16. Black Creek
17. Sinkhole
18. Weigle
19. Deer Creek
20. Marble Pass
21. Sultan Basin
22. 45 Mine
23. Bonanza Queen Spur
24. Williamson Creek
25. Perry Creek
26. Twin Bridges
27. Weden Creek Station
28. Silver Creek
29. Goat Lake
30. Wheeler-Osgood Spur
31. Whitehorse Mountian
32. Jim Creek Route
33. Clinton
34. Smelter

Oso

North Fork Stillaguamish R.

Stillaguamish R.

Arlington

**Seattle & International Railroad
(Northern Pacific Railway)**

South Fork

1st crossing   2nd crossing

Robe

**Lower Robe
Canyon Inset**

Granite
Falls

Pilchuck R.

**Seattle &
Montana
Railway
(Great
Northern
Railway)**

Tulalip

Getchell

Marysville

Hartford

Lake
Stevens

*Lake
Stevens*

Everett

**Seattle Lake Shore & Eastern
(Northern Pacific Railway)**

Whidbey
Island

Possession Snd.

Lowell

**Snohomish,
Skykomish,
and Spokane
Railway**

Snohomish

Snohomish R.

Great Northern Railway

Monroe

Sultan

Puget Sound

N

Edmonds

Brier

Snoqualmier R.

To Seattle

Lake
Washington

Bothell

Woodinville

Duvall

King Co.

Kirkland

0   10 Mi

0   10 Km

©MAPS.COM